AN AFRICAN
IN PARIS

OTHER WORKS BY
BERNARD BINLIN DADIÉ

NOVEL
Climbié (Paris: Éditions Seghers, 1956)

TRAVEL
Patron de New York (Paris: Présence Africaine, 1964)
La Ville où nul ne meurt (Paris: Présence Africaine, 1968)

POETRY
Afrique debout! (Paris: Éditions Seghers, 1950)
La Ronde des jours (Paris: Présence Africaine, 1956)

SHORT STORIES
Commandant Taureault et ses Nègres (Abidjan: Ceda-Hatier, 1980)
Les Jambes du fils de Dieu (Paris: Ceda-Hatier, 1980)

TALES AND POEMS
Hommes de tous les continents (Paris: Présence Africaine, 1967)

TALES
Légendes africaines (Paris: Éditions Seghers, 1954)
Le Pagne noir (Paris: Présence Africaine, 1955)
Contes de Koutou-as-Samala (Paris: Présence Africaine, 1982)

PLAYS
Monsieur Thôgô-gnini (Paris: Présence Africaine, 1970)
Béatrice au Congo (Paris: Présence Africaine, 1971)
Sidi: Maître Escroc; Situation difficile; Serment d'amour (Paris: Présence Africaine,
    1971)
Ils de tempête (Paris: Présence Africaine, 1973)
Mhoi-Ceul (Paris: Présence Africaine, 1979)

AN AFRICAN
IN PARIS

BERNARD BINLIN DADIÉ

Translated by Karen C. Hatch

University of Illinois Press

URBANA AND CHICAGO

Library of Congress
Cataloging-in-Publication Data

Dadié, Bernard Binlin, 1916–
    [Nègre à Paris. English]
    An African in Paris / Bernard Binlin Dadié ; translated
by Karen C. Hatch.
        p.   cm.
    ISBN 0-252-02040-5 (cl.)–ISBN 0-252-06407-0 (pbk.).
    1. Africans—Travel—France—Paris—Fiction. 2. Paris
(France)—Fiction. I. Title.
PQ3989.D28N413   1994
843—dc20   93-30915
                                                CIP

TRANSLATOR'S INTRODUCTION

> On the road to Tomorrow,
> the Road of Men
> The Road of Brothers
> With no other bond but the bond of one for another
> With no other song but the song of one for another
> With no other joy but the joy of one for another . . .
> On the road to Tomorrow,
> The Road of a new world order
> We stand ready.
>
> (Dadié, "Sur la route," in
> *Hommes de tous les continents,* 50)

FORMER minister of culture in the Ivory Coast and one of Africa's most respected fiction writers, poets, and dramatists, Bernard B. Dadié belongs to the older generation of francophone African writers—a generation that includes Birago Diop, well-known Senegalese author of *Les Contes d'Amadou Koumba,* and Léopold Senghor, Senegalese poet and philosopher of Négritude. As children and young adults they knew firsthand the meaning of unquestioned colonial rule. The younger generation, on the other hand—Camara Laye (Guinea), Sembène Ousmane (Senegal), Cheikh Hamidou Kane (Senegal), Mongo Beti, and Ferdinand Oyono (Cameroon), to name a few—was born just prior to the Second World War and grew up during the political unrest of the postwar era, when the clamorings for independence became progressively more heated, and more bitter. With one or two exceptions, the older writers had been born and raised in—or, as in the case of Dadié, educated in—one or the other of the *vieilles communes* of Senegal: Gorée, Dakar, Rufisque, and Saint-Louis. Assimilation was very advanced in the communes, whose inhabitants, irrespective of race, had held French citizenship since 1824 (Brench, "The Novelist's Background," 35). Despite the fact of their citizenship, however, their privileged education, and a basic respect for French culture, the older-generation writers were as deeply committed to the struggle for political and cultural autonomy as the younger; Dadié was, for example, as we will see, a major force behind his country's move toward independence. Anger there was, to be sure, but outright contempt or rejection of the European was not the central issue in this part of Africa—autonomy was. These writers had been simply too involved with the Europeans to have been able to ridicule them with as much success or veracity as the younger writers, who were not so deeply involved with them (Brench, "The Novelist's Background," 36). It is precisely this love-hate relationship with the French that characterizes Dadié's works—indeed, that marks his fundamental "humanism." Ultimately, he is a sharp-witted—amused and amusing—observer of the follies and foibles of us all, and therein lies his true greatness.

*
* *

Dadié was born in Assinie (Ivory Coast) in 1916 and began his career as a writer in the early 1930s while a student at the Ecole Primaire Supérieure de Bingerville (Ivory Coast). Even though he was remote from the Négritude activity then occurring in Paris, his first works celebrated Africa's precolonial past and his own African heritage. Unlike the poet-philosopher Senghor, however, Dadié began by writing dramatic sketches. His first, *Les Villes* (1933), was performed at a children's festival in Abidjan. The next year, he entered the Ecole Normale William Ponty de Gorée (Senegal), where he wrote *Assemien Déhylé,* a chronicle-play about the Agni people and one of its heroic kings (the Agni inhabit the region between the Volta River in Ghana and the Bandama River in the Ivory Coast). Staged by students from the Ivory Coast in 1936 at the Chamber of Commerce in Dakar, it earned enthusiastic reviews. The following year it enjoyed a successful run at the Théâtre des Champs-Elysées in Paris, during the Colonial Exhibition. Dadié's passionate interest in African folklore, history, and legend continued over the next decade, the years of World War II, while he worked in Dakar at the Département de la Bibliotheque et des Archives de l'Institut Français d'Afrique Noire. His first folktales, *Nénuphar reine des eaux* and *Araignée mauvais père,* appeared in the newly created literary review *Dakar jeunes,* and together with the poems of this period they brought him further acclaim (Quillateau, 20). Dadié, however, had not abandoned the stage; after his return to the Ivory Coast in 1947, he produced four

new plays at the Cercle Culturel et Folklorique: *Serment d'amour,*
Situation difficile, Siddi: Maître Escroc, and *Min Adja-Wo.* But his chief
reputation throughout Africa and abroad would be based upon his
poetry, folktales, and, after *Climbié* (1956), his prose fiction.

Dadié's first major collection of poems, *Afrique debout!* was published in Paris by Editions Seghers in 1950. As in most pre-independence
francophone African poetry, his subject is the black-white encounter
and, more specifically, the colonial experience: the invasion of traditional values by an aggressive and alien culture. Although many of the
poems in this collection deal with the mental and physical agony of the
politically oppressed and socially despised black man, others speak
poignantly of a society without racial distinctions or loyalties. In fact,
the dominant theme in the collection is not simply the oppressed black
man but all the oppressed of the world—"Blancs, jaunes, rouges, et
noirs" ("White, yellow, red, and black").

Dadié's humanism ripens in *La Ronde des jours* (1956), his second
volume of poems. In the opening poem, "Les Lignes de nos mains," he
writes:

> The lines of our hands
>> not white
>> not black
>> nor yellow,
> The lines of our hands
> Unite the bouquets of our dreams.
>
> (228)

And in "Le Monde qui nait":

> We will be brothers.
> We will stand united.
> And the stars, in their profusion,
>
> . . . .
>
> Will shine as bright
> As our destiny.
>
> (244)

The very title of Dadié's third major collection of poems, *Hommes*
de tous les continents (1967), suggests its scope and tone. Independence had been a fact in French West Africa for seven years, and Dadié
now addresses himself to all humankind:

Let us join hands
in the dawn of a new day
and say a new prayer.

("Escale dans le temps,"
        July 26, 1965, 90)

The concluding words of the poem "Frère blanc" (1958) are, I think,
the clearest expression of Dadié's ultimate position as a writer, as a
man: "You are a man / I am, too / that says it all" (*Hommes de tous les
continents,* 61).

Perhaps the best summing-up of Dadié's career as a poet is that of
Claude Quillateau: "Once a poet of the oppressed, today a poet of
reconciliation, Bernard Dadié, profoundly Christian, saves what ought
to be saved, that bit of amity which subsists and is enough to keep alive
the one basic feeling behind all mystiques ... the innate love of the
human being spread throughout the universe" (27).

*
* *

Africa's precolonial past is just as important to Dadié as its future. If
many of his poems are serious petitions for a universal community, his
two volumes of folktales—*Légendes africaines* (1954) and *Le Pagne
noir* (1955; translated into English as *The Black Cloth* [1987])—are
efforts to keep alive the art of the oral narrative and the moral values
intrinsic to African folklore. In this respect he is like other francophone
African *"conteurs,"* Birago Diop most notably. The African oral tradition offers a wide variety of story types, ranging from myth and legend
to fairy tales, fables, explanatory tales, and folktales—all with tribal and
historic variations. The line of demarcation between types is, of course,
a fluid one, and the distinctions between story types matter little to
Africans: "What counts for the people is that the characters actually
lived, or that the feats were actually performed" (Dadié, "Le Rôle de la
légende," 167).

In translating traditional oral narratives to the written page, Dadié is
acutely aware of the need to satisfy the demands of divergent audiences:
those who are familiar with the oral performances of a griot and those
who are not. Frequently, of course, he resorts to formulaic openings
and closings, but his descriptions of character and scene are far more
elaborate than those provided by the traditional griot (Tollerson, 82,

92). In Dadié's treatment of Kacou Ananze Spider, for example, the trickster so common in West African folktales, the fixed personality of the oral tale—the "mask," if you will—becomes much more the character of a short story: we not only see the results of his notorious clever cheatings, we are also privy to the machinations of the mind that produced them. The same is true of the scenic descriptions. Yam fields and forests become far more than mere settings; they assume a life of their own—rich, rhythmic lives, filled with sound and symbolic associations.

It may seem ironic that so many African writers in the late 1940s and 1950s should have returned to the ancient oral tradition at the very moment they wished to address a Western audience, share increasingly in Western modes of thinking, and, of course, create a written literature. In another light, the irony was inevitable, and, in truth, not so much an irony at all as one of the honest tensions of experience that an African writer, caught between worlds, was forced to negotiate as best he could. Writers like Birago Diop and Bernard Dadié were determined to salvage the history and wisdom of their own heritage. Storytelling as a natural, regular part of life had declined under colonialism since village life had changed radically. Moreover, in the cities, the values of African collectivism could not be easily continued. The new literature arose out of a collision with the West, bringing with it folk values and a folk "literature" of ancient uniqueness whose worth to the world could only be explored by those who salvaged and reinterpreted it "from within." Not long after the publication of *Le Pagne noir,* Dadié was to write: "We have riches to share. We are no longer in a world where one keeps his wealth, his gifts, to himself. We have something to take to other men, something of ourselves to give them, a wisdom to blend into the wisdom of others" ("Le Rôle de la légende," 173).

* * *

Although French-speaking writers from the Antilles—notably René Maran, Jacques Roumain, and J. S. Alexis—had been publishing novels before the 1940s and continued to do so after the war years, novels of quality by French-speaking Africans did not appear in any number or assume any significance until the 1950s. Camara Laye's autobiographical novel, *L'Enfant noir (The Dark Child),* was the first of these, published in 1953 and awarded the Prix Charles Veillon the following year.

During the next eight years, French presses, responding to the public's increasing interest in the literature of the "Dark Continent," released in quick succession novels by Mongo Beti, Abdoulaye Sadji, Jean Malonga, Ferdinand Oyono, Sembène Ousmane, and Cheikh Hamidou Kane, among others. To many, the years between 1953 and 1961 are still considered the golden age of the novel in francophone African literature.

What characterizes the novels of this period is, inevitably, the content. Virtually all the writers concentrated on one subject alone—Africa—not only as a geographical and political reality but also as a "state of soul" (Moore, x). The hero is almost always black, and the action is usually situated in Africa; but even if the hero is white, as in Camara Laye's *Le Regard du roi* (*The Radiance of the King,* 1954), or the action is set outside Africa, as in Ousmane's *Le Docker noir* (*The Black Docker,* 1956), the story is invariably told from an African perspective, focusing on specifically African problems. The novelists of the 1950s are, without exception, politically and artistically committed to the anticolonial struggle, and, by and large, their works are constructed around one central theme: the disintegration of their familiar society under the impact of colonialism and the attendant consciousness of loss, loneliness, disillusionment, prejudice, and brutality.

Dadié's first long work of prose fiction, *Climbié,* was written in 1953, when the author was thirty-seven years old; it appeared the same year as young Beti's *Le Pauvre Christ de Bomba* (*The Poor Christ of Bomba*) and Oyono's *Une Vie de boy* (*Houseboy*) and *Le Vieux nègre et la médaille* (*The Old Man and the Medal*). While it has touches of the bitterness found in both Beti and Oyono, the bitterness is softened by humor, sanely balanced and discriminating, and subordinate to a Catholic humanism, a ripe maturity of mind and heart hardly, if at all, evident in the younger writers. Dadié is without the pessimistic bleakness of Beti—"*Climbié*" means, after all, "someday"—and his hope for a better world is much firmer than the timid gestures toward it at the end of Oyono's *Le Vieux nègre et la médaille*.

Dadié also has a firmer sense of history and of continuity in African life despite colonialism. Moreover, unlike his younger peers from the Cameroon, he actually participated in the struggle for independence. Dadié's father, Gabriel Dadié, was among the early founders, along with Houphouet-Boigny, of the Rassemblement Démocratique Africain (RDA), the chief political party for the independence movement throughout West Africa. At age thirty, Dadié himself was writing anticolonial articles for *Le Reveil,* the party's chief newspaper, and in February

1949, as a result of his work with the Partie Démocratique de la Côte d'Ivoire (a branch of the RDA), he was arrested and thrown into prison (Mayes, 3). The actual sentencing did not come until March 1950, when, to a storm of public protest, Dadié, along with Coffi Gadeau, Jean-Baptiste Mockey, Seri Koré, Philippe Viera, Mathieu Ekra, Jacob William, and Albert Paraiso (all members of the RDA's board of directors), appeared before the court. Dadié was sentenced to three years in prison, most of the others to five (Clérici, 118). The following lines, written immediately after his arrest, reveal, as do his other writings, a passionate belief in the right of every human being to be treated with dignity:

From my window, I watched people going and coming on the sidewalks and streets: people and cars free to go where they pleased. I heard the noise and saw the smiles; I saw also the rays of the sun dancing merrily on the leaves. Never before had I truly appreciated what freedom meant than at this moment when that fundamental right of all people was taken from me. The police commissioner hurried to close the window and said to me: "You are a prisoner. You no longer have the right to look outside." That bridge connecting me to the sun, to the crowds, to the lives of all those who are free was destroyed. . . . I was a man without rights, an object, nothing more than a plaything in the hands of others, a mouse trapped in the claws of a cat. . . .

After we were searched, we were led to cell number 16, where we were made to lie down on the bare ground. I could hear the rattle of the guns, the guards talking to one another in the prison yard. The sun, as if to make fun of the bars on the window, managed to send us that portion of light reserved just for us. The continuous gusts of wind acted as though they wanted to remove a huge veil. . . .

At noon, Zougrana, the cook, shouted: "Grand-Bassam—line up!" Like chickens ready to be thrown a bit of corn, the half-starved prisoners, ragged and in tatters, raced up from all sides, shoving, clinging to each other, each armed with a small basket that would serve as a plate. Zougrana reached into a barrel and began throwing bits of yam. We were forced to catch them in air, like dogs chasing after bones. . . .

The constant bang of cell doors slamming shut seemed to say: "People have a right to more respect, people have a right to more respect" (in Clérici, 119–20).[1]

1. Dadié's prison diary was published under the title *Carnet de prison* (1980).

Dadié's arrest and imprisonment are treated with sad but unbitter reticence in the last part of *Climbié,* part II. Despite his inside experience in the anticolonial struggle, perhaps because of it, Dadié pictures the Europeans with much more objectivity and balance than do Beti and Oyono. If the twenty-year-old judge who imprisons Climbié is shown for the callow, blind squirt that he is, he is more than balanced by the respectful portrait of Targe, the European photographer, whose letter to Climbié ends the book with a plea for brotherhood. Europeans are portrayed precisely and unsparingly in their profiteering mentality, their prejudices and fantasies, their fears of Africa, and their blind overreliance on technology and business to ensure "civilization"; but the portraits are many-dimensional and, as it were, egalitarian. Dadié is most like the younger novelists in the quality of his African laughter, as, of course, he is in the courage and artistic intelligence such laughter required in 1953.

Climbié, however, is not a novel in the usual sense of the term; nor does Dadié consider himself a novelist. It is, more accurately, a *récit,* "a sum of things," as he once described it to me.[2] The *récit* takes the form of a series of vignettes, each one complete in itself yet intimately tied to all the others. In scenic structure and visual acuity, Dadié's style has many of the qualities of Maupaussant, whom he greatly admired; even in his language, though highly evocative and close to poetry, there is much of the classical precision and sobriety of the master French realist. The central character in all of Dadié's major prose works (*Climbié, Un Nègre à Paris, Patron de New York,* and *La Ville où nul ne meurt*) is more nearly a persona than a fictional hero, a doer and sufferer close to Dadié himself (but, of course, not quite identical)—a character who examines the manners and customs of another people (French, Americans, Italians) and then compares them to his own, all for the purpose of, as Dadié explains, "discerning the differences and similarities from the perspective of a universal humanism" (in Quillateau, 152). There is fiction in his works but not much make-believe. His purest fiction perhaps is Climbié—an autobiographical off-slipping of Dadié himself, yes, but at the same time a distanced character, or vehicle, for exploring and rendering experience. Climbié is a simple clerk (as Dadié never was), an average *évolué* in the colonial society of French West Africa.

Climbié has been out of print for some time now, but because the issues Dadié explores in this book—brotherhood, equality and justice,

2. Interview with Dadié, Paris, November 24, 1968.

and a sense of fair play whatever one's color or origins—are those also explored in *Un Nègre à Paris,* a few words regarding the earlier work seem in order. Moreover, it may be argued that the more confident, certainly more jovial narrator of *Un Nègre à Paris* (this work was published on the eve of independence) was the natural successor to the more youthful, more politically self-absorbed Climbié. Dadié's narrator, it may be said, grew up, and in the process broadened his vision and developed a far more penetrating sense of humor.

In *Climbié,* Dadié describes the everyday life of a young African boy from the Ivory Coast. The child grows up; the student passes his exams; the young man secures employment in Dakar and then returns home, where he becomes actively involved in the movement for independence. The work is divided into two parts: part I focuses on Climbié's childhood and education, part II on his career as a young man, his life during and following World War II, when the cries for independence came into the open. Like Camara Laye in *L'Enfant noir,* Dadié begins in the village and moves outward to a modern metropolis (Dakar instead of Conakry), but whereas Laye has the Dark Child board a plane for France in the end, Dadié brings his young hero almost, but not quite, full circle, back to the land of his birth. Step by step, Climbié passes from the world of Ebrié village tradition, to life in French schools, then by sea voyage to the modern urban world of bureaucracy and politics before returning, again by sea, to Abidjan, a smaller replica of the Senegalese city and the capital of the Ivory Coast. By sketching the joys and wonders of village boyhood as a backdrop for Climbié's loop of adventure, Dadié is able to dramatize the shock of a sensibility uprooted by Europeanized education. Climbié, like the Dark Child, is deeply attached to the African traditions that gave meaning to his boyhood, and separation from them only serves to focus all the more powerfully for the adult the value of what he has lost.

The significant moments in Climbié's childhood all occur with members of his extended African family. When his uncle N'dabian dies, Climbié's second uncle, Assouan Koffi, assumes responsibility for him. Koffi, a civil servant, appears at a crucial point early in Climbié's schoolboy career to show his young nephew pictures of Harlem riots. Climbié cannot fully understand what he sees in the photographs, nor can he understand why his uncle's picture book is censored literature for Africans; but, for the first time, he is aware that the struggle for human rights is not confined to Africa alone, that no matter where the black man lives, he lives in chains—something neither church nor school had taught him. Later in the book Climbié visits Assouan Koffi while on vacation from school, and he discovers that his uncle has made a valiant attempt to return to the soil. We took the wrong road from the start, he tells Climbié. "The European was a ruler, a very powerful lord who had his prison, who levied taxes. . . . And you had to live in his wake, in his shadow, in order to have a little piece" (88). "To be a farmer is not easy," he continues, "[but] at least you have your independence. And that means a great deal in the life of a man" (92). "Work! and after the work, independence, my child! To be the responsibility of no one! That should be the motto of your generation. You must always shun the man who doesn't like to work" (89).

Climbié, however, does not return to the soil, despite the hopes of his uncle Assouan. He is pulled away from this life by the same unknown, all-powerful forces that gradually uprooted the Dark Child from his native village of Kouroussa. Throughout part II of the book, Climbié looks back periodically with nostalgia upon the joys of a lost world, of fresh air, freedom, and healthy African laughter—"this laughter which is not made for a drawing room . . . and still less for an air-conditioned hotel, where it wilts and dies" (127). He becomes, and knows that he has become, only one more of the multitude of Africans who exchange the pure invigorating air of the country for the dusty, overheated air of the city. In leaving the land against his uncle's warning, Climbié loses some depth of himself.

Structurally, *Climbié* is a progression of scenic tableaux whose interlocking motifs of flight, guilt, bewilderment, and loneliness keep us inside the mind of a protagonist who suffers more than he acts. The story of Climbié is that of a sensibility adrift in a world in which something is always missing and which keeps reflecting back to the sufferer his own isolation. Significantly, Climbié's moments of intimacy are few, and when they happen they are almost always shadowed by some kind of reflective constraint and confusion of feeling. The childhood evenings in the lap of his uncle N'dabian are the only moments of physical contact in the book, and the farther Climbié travels away from them, the lonelier he becomes.

Another conflict in the book and, of course, in Climbié's experience, is that of Europe and Africa. In scene after scene, the two worlds are juxtaposed: on one side, the European residential quarter with its hard-shelled houses, on the other, the African village with its huts. The two confront each other but never join. The behavior of the Europeans amuses the Africans, as that of the Africans baffles the Europeans—

something that Montaigne too had noticed some four centuries earlier. In part I, for example, Dadié dramatizes their differences by describing their respective reactions to a threatened epidemic of yellow fever (which, however, never comes to pass). The whites panic, declare a quarantine, veil themselves during the day, and sleep tensely under mosquito netting at night. The Africans blithely continue to sleep in the open—it is too hot inside the huts—and break the silence of the quarantine with their drums. In part II, however, such differences are usually treated with less humor. With the coming of World War II, the Africans began to question Western civilization sharply: What would white men be without their guns and cannons? Is their civilization so fragile that they must conserve it by armed force? In the "primitive" past, men fought for a piece of land or a water hole; in the Europeanized present, they fight for Liberty, Justice, and Civilization with weapons of mass death. Where is the progress, and what can such abstractions mean to exploited Africans?

Climbié is haunted by such questions—and by the mounting weight of his experience with European blindness. As he remarks once to Dassi, a young Togolese he meets on a bus, Europeans walk into an office full of African clerks, then turn around and leave, saying, "There's no one here" (122). In general, the Africans' response is optimistic. They turn their backs and laugh among themselves; even in prison they smile. The constant smiling baffles the European jailers, but, as Climbié comes to see, it is a means of survival.

In the postwar era, as Dadié renders it, the color barriers are pragmatically relaxed and attitudes changed; yet the two worlds remain as far apart as ever. The few whites whose change of heart is authentic are like conscientious objectors in a society that now studies the "new" African as one might a rock or a plant—an object of curiosity. Climbié is befriended by the European photographer Targe; yet their different worlds, at that moment in history, preclude any lasting friendship. And when Climbié begins writing anticolonial articles, he is thrown into prison. Open criticism of the colonial regime still provokes a brutal repression from most whites. In the strike by railroad workers (and by clerks) in part II, Dadié, however, dramatizes the beginning of the change among Africans from smiling passivity to angry action.

Despite moments of anger, distrust, and frustration, Climbié cannot bring himself to hate Europeans; indeed, his inability to hate is another source of conflict. Though they have pulled him away from his roots, they have also given him a "higher" religion, a training in thought, and a literary heritage. Climbié's love for literature is shown early in his schoolboy career when he prefers browsing in the French bookstore SACO to playing games. At first, books are little more than colorful titles and jackets, but they become a passion. By part II, Climbié can tell Dassi that Africans must read more than any other people in the world, for they are precisely at the crossing-point of two civilizations. The only way for them to be up to date, to hold their own in a society that refuses to assist them, is to frequent bookstores and libraries. Later, however, after he returns to the Ivory Coast, Climbié tries to sell his books when he realizes that only money has a voice in present civilization; but no matter how hard he tries, he keeps putting aside one book as not for sale, then another, until finally he is forced into self-knowledge. French education also gives Climbié, very early in life, an awareness of African history, past and present. In part I, for example, as he walks around the historic island of Gorée, the stopping-off point for slave-traders, he imagines those who cried out for mercy, in pain, as they waited in their cells to be shipped off to the Americas. Yes, he thinks to himself, Gorée, like the whole of Africa, is still a depot. The white man continues to rob Africa of her riches and to replace them, at best, with only second-hand goods and machines. "I beg you, do not send us any more machines; send us men instead" (in Quillateau, 23), Dadié once pleaded.

What holds *Climbié* together is not Dadié's ridicule of mechanized white society, however, but his passionate preoccupation with justice. All suffering people—black, white, red, or yellow—have the right to dignity and respect as human beings. Dadié's humanism owes something to Victor Hugo, whom, like Maupassant, he admired and respected for different reasons. "As for Victor Hugo, I liked *Les Misérables* very much, for its realism and the moral philosophy that Jean Valjean works out. One cannot help but be taken with Hugo: he stirs up so many ideas, he sees so far and deep, his vision of life is so cosmic, so dynamic" (in Quillateau, 150–51). Even when his ridicule of the European is harsh, Dadié always assumes that the races, although diverse, make only one small bouquet in the cosmos, and that—someday—"its pleasant fragrance will fill the universe when every individual has found a place in the community" (*Climbié,* 114). In the meantime, African drums, ringing out their ancient rhythms, symbolize an African defense against the modern abyss of depersonalization. It is significant that Dadié gives the closing words in *Climbié* to the European Targe, who, in a letter to Climbié, writes, "following the example of our explorers, I say that we must go forward and boldly map out the paths that the new caravans will follow, the caravans of fraternity in a world at peace" (189). The dignity and freedom of every human being is the final affirmation. Climbié is and will remain a black African, but he understands, as Dadié himself once remarked, that wherever there is suffering among black people, "the Negro should ungrudgingly offer a hand to all his enemies: he should say to himself that all men suffer, and that those who take delight in doing evil are simply incomplete human beings" (in Quillateau, 27).

*
* *

On August 7, 1960, Dadié's homeland became independent. On November 27, Houphouet-Boigny was named president of the new Republique de Côte d'Ivoire, and shortly afterward, Bernard Dadié became Directeur des Beaux-Arts et de la Recherche (Rougerie, 105), a position he held until just recently. The year just prior to independence, however, turned out to be an equally important year in the history of African literature, for it was then that Présence Africaine published Dadié's *Un Nègre à Paris,* the first work to be set outside Africa where an African is shown in every respect as the equal of Europeans. Moreover, it is a work that, according to Janis Mayes, "introduces a new literary genre into African literature: the 'chronique'" (Mayes, 5), wherein "Dadié adapts traditional African values to the modern world and fuses the two in a new reality" (Mayes, 8). Dadié was to continue with this genre in two subsequent works: *Patron de New York* (1964) and *La Ville où nul ne meurt* (1968). But, as Mayes also points out, Dadié's "chroniques" do not adhere to the generally accepted definition of the term. The sequence of events in each is not chronological; nor are the events themselves without philosophic or literary commentary. "The material which serves as the basis for these works was gathered during two separate trips made by Dadié: one in 1959 to Paris and Rome, and the other in 1964 to New York. None of the works was actually written at the time of the trips. Neither do those dates which appear at the end of each chronique (July 14–August 2, 1956, for *Un Nègre à Paris;* March 18, 1963, for *Patron de New York;* March 24–April 3, 1959, for *La Ville où nul ne meurt* [Rome]) correspond to the actual dates of his travels" (Mayes, 5). Events are carefully selected, and with one purpose in mind: to cultivate "an appreciation for the components of one's own culture through critical comparisons and contrasts with similar components of foreign cultures" (Mayes, 6). The ways in which Dadié calls up the events, however, as well as the free and easy manner with which he treats them cannot help but remind one of the fictional techniques employed by Montesquieu in his *Persian Letters* (1721)—a fact that has not gone unnoticed by at least three of Dadié's early commentators: M. and S. Battestini, Roger Mercier, and A. C. Brench, and most recently by Elizabeth Mudimbe-Boyi. The author's "irrepressible wit," his keenly critical philosophic reflections on the customs and mores of the Parisians, and, as Brench remarks, "his unshakeable belief in Africans' equality with other men . . . make him possibly the best writer from Africa to be the first explorer in Paris" (Brench, *The Novelist's Inheritance,* 87). They make him also very much like Montesquieu's Persian visitors. There are, however, important differences.

Montesquieu was working within a long-standing tradition when the first edition of *Persian Letters* made its appearance (unsigned) in Amsterdam in 1721. As G. L. Van Roosbroeck noted some years ago, "foreign observers" as well as "pseudo-foreign letters" were both well-established and widespread fictional devices by the time Montesquieu launched his Persians, Rica and Usbek, on a spirited critique of the society of his day. "Foreign observers" as critics of European life and society appear as far back as the fourteenth century, in the satirical poem *Apparicion Maistre Jehan de Meun,* by Honoré Bonet, and they continue to make their appearance in the mid-seventeenth century, notably in Baltasar Gracían's *El Criticón* (1650–53) and Ferrante Pallavicino's *Il Divorzio celeste* (1649) (Van Roosbroeck, 22–35).

Closer in time to Montesquieu, and arguably, therefore, more of a likely influence on him, were the following extraordinarily popular works: *Letters of a Turkish Spy* (1684), by the Genoese-in-exile Giovanni Paolo Marana (after the appearance of a French translation in the same year, printings of Marana's work followed in rapid succession, with additional volumes added by other writers); Dufresny's *Amusements sérieux et comiques* (1699); various "pseudo-foreign" letters published in editions of the *Spectator* and the *Tatler* between May 13, 1710, and June 21, 1714; and, most significantly, according to Van Roosbroeck, J. F. Bernard's *Reflexions morales, satiriques et comiques sur les moeurs de notre siècle* (1711), which included numerous letters by a "Persian Philosopher" detailing his impressions of Europe and the Europeans (Van Roosbroeck 42–63). Thus, by the time Montesquieu's *Persian Letters* saw its first printing, the mask of a "pseudo foreigner" had already established its credentials as a powerful critical device: "This mask—at first mainly badinage, as in Dufresny's *Amusements sérieux et comiques,*—powerfully helped the authors in depersonalizing their mental attitude and in endowing them with a certain freshness of judgment which allowed them to survey Western culture and prejudices with the naive and censorious eye of a contemplative Oriental" (Van Roosbroeck, 82–83). And nothing significant was to escape that "naive and censorious eye": neither the sheer diversity of human life and the hypocrisy of individuals and institutions, nor the misguided intentions and perverted values of either, or both.

Montesquieu's work enjoyed enormous popularity, so much so, in fact, that the "pseudo-foreign letter" continued in vogue to a greater or lesser degree throughout the eighteenth century. Even Voltaire was to capitalize on its success with his *Lettres d'Amabed,* which appeared in 1769 (Battestini, Battestini, and Mercier, 56). Clearly, Dadié was well acquainted with the genre. Even more to the point, he revived the form in *Un Nègre à Paris,* but with significant innovations. As a result, one must thank Dadié for creating something substantially new—not merely a special type of "chronique," but an "epistolary chronique," or, perhaps more simply, a "chronique" in the style of a foreign letter. Tradition and innovation seem perfectly fused—effortlessly so—and the fun of reading *Un Nègre à Paris* comes, I think, from listening ever more closely to the voice of one who recalls the past (his own and that of the Parisians) in order to define his identity for the future. The French assimilated Dadié, but Dadié also assimilated the French—their language, literature, and history—and, in the process, became a shrewd critic of the very France that had purposed to absorb him. A critic, yes, but one who will be forever drawn to the magical city of Paris: "no one," he says at the end of *Un Nègre à Paris,* "absolutely no one, can resist her call."

Whereas Montesquieu's *Persian Letters* is the correspondence of several Persians, on a visit to Europe, with each other and their friends back home in Isfahan, Dadié's *Un Nègre à Paris* is one continuous letter, not a dramatic interchange. Moreover, in Montesquieu's work, there are two principal writers: Rica, the younger and more light-hearted of the two, and Usbek, older, more serious, and generally more reflective. Each, of course, represents a side of Montesquieu's own nature (Davidson, 9–15). Dadié, on the other hand, works with a single persona, Tanhoé Bertin, who is writing to a friend back home in Africa; we discover right off his ability to move quickly and easily between playful commentary and penetrating analysis. A perfect instance of this "combined vision" occurs as his plane passes over the meticulously plotted farmland of France on its slow descent into Orly Airport. Dadié writes, "For sure this land must be ruled by a people who toe the mark, a square and chalk-line in their minds and eyes. Phenomenal creatures, these people; they're all in love with the perfectly straight line. . . . It looks as though they even prune their weeds" (this volume, p. 14). In the next breath we hear, "For them, life must follow its usual course; everything in its proper channel. . . . Get off the beaten path—that's what I say. They're an old people with old habits, but life stays young only if you're thrown off course now and then" (p. 14). In another scene, toward the end of the work, we hear of his need to buy a good raincoat (all Parisians have one) before he leaves the city. He encounters one smiling salesperson after another—the one who actually sells him the raincoat is extremely attentive—and then, when it comes time to pay, a cashier refuses at first to accept his traveler's check (it is accepted only after he shows an identity card and provides an address). "The Parisians are always on guard," he writes. "They never take anything at face value" (p. 148).

Almost every scene in the "letter" progresses in like manner: first, the quick, penetrating—and often irrepressibly witty—picture of the Parisians in action or attitude; then, the moment of reflection followed by a more generalized statement, a "truth," so to speak, which the designedly naive Tanhoé Bertin believes he has discovered. Often, of course, these "truths" border on the cliché—for example, the Parisians' love of cats, fortune-tellers, flowers, and especially their own history—but what makes each observation seem new are the continual comparisons with his own world back home. At one point, for example, Tanhoé says,

the longer I study . . . the Parisians, the more I realize how much their ancestors resembled ours. The Parisians would like to argue the point, but they won't, not because it just might be true, but because I seem to be taking them backward, forgetting in one fell swoop the thousands and thousands of years of hard work they've put in to get where they are now. . . . Why it's enough to make me laugh! If they were as old as they think they are, their skin would have darkened with age. But they're barely even tan! . . . Of course, the sun has continued to do its work, since it has changed the color of some peoples' hair to brown. And who knows, maybe some day . . . No! We'd better not scare them! (pp. 85–86)

Parisian men, he continues, have obviously "developed a taste for the color red" (they can't resist smiling, beckoning lips), but they haven't, as yet, learned to love the color black. "What, I ask you, would we do in their place? . . . But let's not throw stones, since we're men too" (p. 86). The moment concludes in a way that's recognizably Dadié's: with an awareness that all people share certain weaknesses.

We don't know why Tanhoé goes to Paris. As he says early on, "I'm not famous. I'm neither a chief nor the president of an organization. . . . And I certainly don't have a commission. Let's face it, I represent nothing" (p. 4). We know only that he has been given a ticket and that he is eager to see, not the Paris others wanted him to see, but the Paris he wants to see. And this is just as well, for Dadié's free-wheeling style and tone would not accommodate a more serious, more traditionally didactic mission. If the ultimate purpose of the visit is to unmask the Parisians by catching them off guard, to get beyond the cliché and see them for what they truly are—as quirky as the rest of humankind—then Tanhoé's visit must maintain a certain spontaneity. Parisians move fast, as we hear over and over again, and Tanhoé must move fast too. That, in many ways, explains the randomness of his letter. He will see something, stop for a moment to comment on it, then wander off in another direction—his eyes trying to absorb as much as they can in the space of two weeks. Frequently he will return to an idea or event he mentioned long before, and when he does the original "vision" takes on new dimensions. In many ways, therefore, both the pace and structure of the letter correspond to Tanhoé's description of the metro, his favorite "monument"—the one becoming, thereby, the mirror image of the other.

> When you arrive in Paris . . . be sure to get yourself a map of the metro. Another wasted expense, but get one anyway. Armed with this map, proceed to lose yourself in the maze of corridors and arrows, of signs and crowds and wrong ways, ascents and descents; don't get on the train you should but the one you shouldn't; then go into another station, exit, enter again . . . take off and lose yourself once more. . . . You'll even learn the shortcuts in time. (p. 35)

When he later returns to his favorite subject ("that enormous underground spiderweb that lures everyone"), the tone becomes more somber. Gone are the corridors and arrows, the entrances and exits that marked his initial encounter; they have been replaced by images of those "who built the marvels we're forever admiring but who are lost in the pages of history." "They worked by the sweat of their brows," Tanhoé writes, "but their names never manage to appear on a monument. And yet, they're what fame and glory are built on; because of them we're able to do what we do" (p. 56). Parisians may not always remember those nameless masses who built their glittering monuments and gave them the freedoms they now enjoy, but, as Tanhoé reminds us, the city continues to welcome "to her bosom all the disinherited of the earth" (p. 82).

During his meanderings through Paris, Tanhoé notes every vital detail of what he sees with absolute precision. With quick, deft strokes, he shows Parisians as he finds them—lounging in cafes, looking at their watch as they hurry along, eating with their hands—an intricate procedure with its own rules of etiquette, of course. Their cavalier blood is made apparent when they meet face to face on the street, in hotels, restaurants, or shops, as they engage in minutes upon minutes of *je vous en prie*'s and *après vous*'s. Some of his most telling descriptions are of Parisian women, their makeup and hairstyles, the way they light a cigarette, their eyes, their lips. He comments on taxis and pedestrians, and the near-collisions that never happen. He reflects on the importance of newspapers in everyday life, the frightening amount of salt the people use, and their absolute determination to keep their language "pure" and unsullied. The list is endless. At the same time he is doing all this, he is also evoking the shadows of history, juxtaposing live Parisians with their heritage. The celebration of July 14, for example, illicits a rather lengthy description of the Parisians' democratic fervor and patriotism for the flag, then fades immediately into a discussion of their medieval ancestors. Saint Geneviève (the city's patron saint), Abelard and Eloise, Marat, Mirabeau, Talleyrand, and Napoleon—they're all here, and many others besides.

Perhaps the most important "shadow" to make an appearance, however, is the "jongleur," that vagabond satirist of days gone by who lived on the margin of society and sang for his money, the ancestor of all writers, Tanhoé says, those "who should lead us toward the light" (p. 78). Although the reference to the "jongleur" is made in the context of a rather biting criticism of the role journalists play in contemporary French society (that "race of wasp-masons, who, with a mere flutter of their wings, can topple an entire political system" and who, "if your views conflict with theirs," "will strip you naked" "and expose you to the full glare of the sun"—pp. 75–76). Tanhoé himself is, in many ways, like those traveling minstrels of the past, or, as Mayes argues, a twentieth-century griot (Mayes, 7) intent on recreating —and thus preserving—the role of the traditional African storyteller.

He too must travel unknown areas, where who-knows-what surprises (good or bad) lie in wait, and he too controls the world he's writing about and conducts the song that, for him, is Paris. One lengthy bitter sting, and his letter would be the worst sort of invective; a steady dose of good-natured humor, however, and we find raillery at its finest. This, I believe, is what Dadié hoped to achieve in the voice and vision of Tanhoé Bertin. Parisians are neither better nor worse than anyone else; they're just different. Like the flowers they so adore, the Parisians too have their thorns; they may not always let you touch them, but if you make an honest effort to tune into what they say, those thorns will occasionally retract—and at the oddest moments, Tanhoé discovers.

Dadié's narrator, who leaves for Paris "with the eyes of all [his] friends and relatives" and who is determined to "take everything in" has, without explicitly saying so, created a mission for himself—he's off to discover "the Other," as Mudimbe-Boyi so aptly states, "other human beings with whom one can communicate" (Mudimbe-Boyi, 34)—and his experiences will not only belong to him but to all those who share in the journey, readers included. The Other, once indicative of those who weren't white, who, by Western standards, were frequently considered "culturally inferior," has shifted reference (Mudimbe-Boyi, 31–32). But even more to the point, by unmasking the Other through firsthand experience and showing that Other to be fundamentally no different from anyone else, Dadié has successfully broken through the cultural and political barriers that, to a greater or lesser extent, separate us all. Well, almost.

As his two-week stay comes to a close, Tanhoé discovers that despite all his walking and looking he still doesn't really know the people or their city: "No, my friend, this country that creates new songs and a complete new repertory of dance steps with each passing season doesn't let itself be known as easily as one might think. You can't begin to budge those old gray stones, and you certainly can't treat these people as though you're one of them. They've had time to figure out who they are and can present whatever face they want whenever they want" (p. 127). In the end, Paris remains a mystery. Dadié would allude to this again, this time in his poem "Paris pour moi," written on July 20, 1960, not long after the publication of *Un Nègre à Paris:*

Paris
For some,

Is an endless round of glittering festivity,
A perennial fairyland.

For me, Paris will always be
　A mirage in the wilderness
　The enigmatic smile on the faces of the old,
　The enigmatic heart of a woman.

(Hommes de tous les continents, 27)

Un Nègre à Paris is, I suggest, not simply a "chronique," nor an "epistolary chronique"; it is the song of a twentieth-century "jongleur" who happens to be African. Dadié's work, therefore, is as much a turning point in the history of literature written in French as it is a milestone in the literature of modern Africa. We have only to consider the number of travel narratives subsequently written by Africans who have also chosen to cast their eyes on the European—most notably Blaise N'Djehoya and Massaer Diallo in *Un Regard noir* (1984) to truly appreciate Dadié's position as a writer and critic. Indeed, *Un Nègre à Paris* not only introduced a new genre into African literature but gave birth to a whole school of travel writing as well.

*

*　*

A word regarding the translation. In Letter CXXIX of Montesquieu's *Persian Letters,* Rica tells Usbek of a conversation that ensued between a geometer and a translator after they had collided with each other outside a coffeehouse. The translator says, " 'I am very glad you ran against me, for I have great news to tell you: I have just published my Horace.' 'How!' exclaimed the geometer, 'it is two thousand years since Horace was published. . . . ' 'Do you not think that I have done the public a great service in making them familiar with good authors?' 'I am not so sure of that. . . . Translations are like copper money, which have quite the same value as a gold piece, and are even of greater use among the people; but they are base coin and always light' " (in Davidson, 283–84). I can only hope that *An African in Paris* is neither base nor light. Most especially do I hope that the translation (even in some small way) lives up to the review of the original appearing in the *Abidjan-Matin,* April 20, 1960: "The entire work is a gift made expressly for Paris, for France; every detail along the way illustrates his [Dadié's] firm conviction that someday all men of good will, will come together and learn to understand and love each other."

ACKNOWLEDGMENTS

I would like to thank Ed and my parents for their great, good faith and undying courage; Palmer and John for their support and encouragement; and the editors at Présence Africaine for kindly agreeing to several extensions. I am in your debt.

WORKS CITED

Battestini, M., S. Battestini, and Roger Mercier. *Bernard Dadié: Ecrivain Ivoirien*. Paris: Fernand Nathan, 1964.

Beti, Mongo. *Le Pauvre Christ de Bomba*. Paris: Éditions Robert Laffont, 1956.

Brench, A. C. "The Novelist's Background in French Colonial Africa," *African Forum* 3, no. 1 (Summer 1967): 34–41.

———. *The Novelist's Inheritance in French Africa*. London: Oxford University Press, 1967.

Clérici, André, ed. *Histoire de la Côte d'Ivoire*. Abidjan: CEDA, 1962.

Dadié, Bernard B. *Afrique debout!* in *Bernard B. Dadié: Légendes et poèmes*. Paris: Éditions Seghers, 1966.

———. *Carnet de prison*. Abidjan: CEDA, 1980.

———. *Climbié*. Paris: Éditions Seghers, 1956. (*Climbié*. Trans. Karen C. Chapman [Hatch]. London: Heinemann Educational Books, 1971; New York: Africana Publishing, 1971.)

———. *Hommes de tous les continents*. Paris: Présence Africaine, 1967.

———. *Légendes africaines*. Paris: Éditions Seghers, 1954.

———. *Un Nègre à Paris*. Paris: Présence Africaine, 1959.

———. *Le Pagne noir*. Paris: Présence Africaine, 1955. (*The Black Cloth*. Trans. Karen C. Hatch. Amherst: University of Massachusetts Press, 1987.)

———. *Patron de New York*. Paris: Présence Africaine, 1964.

———. "Le Rôle de la légende dans la culture populaire des Noirs d'Afrique," *Présence Africaine* 14–15 (June–September 1957): 165–74.

———. *La Ronde des jours* (1956), in *Bernard B. Dadié: Légendes et poèmes*. Paris: Éditions Seghers, 1966.

———. *La Ville où nul ne meurt*. Paris: Présence Africaine, 1968.

Davidson, John, trans. *The Persian Letters,* by Montesquieu. London: George Routledge and Sons, n.d.

Diop, Birago. *Les Contes d'Amadou Koumba.* Paris: Fasquelle, 1947; Paris: Présence Africaine, 1961.

Laye, Camara. *L'Enfant noir.* Paris: Librairie Plon, 1953.

———. *Le Regard du roi.* Paris: Librairie Plon, 1954.

Mayes, Janis A., trans. *The City Where No One Dies (La Ville où nul ne meurt),* by Bernard B. Dadié. Washington, D.C.: Three Continents Press, 1986.

Moore, Gerald. *Seven African Writers.* London: Oxford University Press, 1962.

Mudimbe-Boyi, Elizabeth. "Travel, Representation, and Difference; or, How Can One Be a Parisian?" Trans. Mildred Mortimer. *Research in African Literatures* 23, no. 3 (Autumn 1992): 25–39.

N'Djehoya, Blaise, and Massaer Diallo. *Un Regard noir.* Paris: Autrement, 1984.

Ousmane, Sembène. *Le Docker noir.* Paris: Éditions Debresse, 1956.

Oyono, Ferdinand. *Une Vie de boy.* Paris: Collection *Lettres Nouvelle,* Julliard, 1956.

———. *Le Vieux nègre et la médaille.* Paris: Collection *Lettres Nouvelle,* Julliard, 1956.

Quillateau, Claude. *Bernard B. Dadié: L'Homme et l'oeuvre.* Paris: Présence Africaine, 1967.

Rougerie, Gabriel. *La Côte d'Ivoire.* Paris: Presses Universitaires de France, 1967.

Tollerson, Marie S. *Mythology and Cosmology in the Narratives of Bernard Dadié and Birago Diop: A Structural Approach.* Washington, D.C.: Three Continents Press, 1984.

Van Roosbroeck, G. L. *Persian Letters before Montesquieu.* Rpt. New York: Burt Franklin, 1972.

AN AFRICAN
IN PARIS

GOOD NEWS, my friend, good news! I have a ticket to Paris . . . yes, Paris! The very same Paris we've so often talked and dreamed about! I'll be leaving in a few days. Even I will finally be able to see Paris with my own eyes. From now on, I'll be a little like the rest of the world—I too will wear the halo and smell of perfume, the halo and perfume of Paris. I too will touch those walls and trees and meet the people.

I can hardly believe it myself. And yet, I assure you, it's true. Just look here, here in my pocket, you'll see the ticket. ONE roundtrip ticket. To convince myself that all this is real, I'm forever taking the ticket out, examining it, and putting it back again. I can't begin to tell you how many times I've done this since yesterday when it was handed to me. But I'll keep on doing it until it's tired and begs for mercy. Sometimes all I do is touch it, to make sure it's there, where it should be, to make sure it hasn't flown away, to make sure . . .

You know as well as I do that it's not every day one has a ticket to Paris. You have to "be somebody" to go there, and, as you and I both know, I'm not "somebody." For me this ticket is more than a sweet-smelling, beautifully written love letter in which a special someone smothers me with "huge, warm kisses" and assures me she will always love me, that she misses me. How I wish you'd been with me so that, together, we could have read the information on the ticket—as we used to do just a short time ago with letters we received. People would have laughed as they walked by us, and the two of us would have laughed right along with them. But this ticket doesn't have the sort of perfume we can inhale—that kind comes from a sweetheart. We can't even look between the lines to see where a heart skipped a beat or where someone stopped to catch her breath.

No! This ticket was issued robot-like by a secretary anxious to hear the noonday bell; she had other fish to fry, other concerns all her own. There was no special message inside, not a single sigh. So much for that! The main thing is, it's mine, and it's going to take me to Paris! And you can be sure I'll keep a good grip on it so it won't fall out. That reminds me . . . at first I couldn't decide just where to keep it—in the desk? A drawer? A trunk? A suitcase? In my pocket? If I did that, it might fall out.

As you can tell, keeping the ticket safe became a real problem for me. I finally decided to keep it on me—just the same as if it were a religious medal or a good-luck charm. It's right there, in my pocket, and I keep touching it as though it had special powers. It keeps me warm, it invigorates me . . . I'd give anything to be able to take your eyes with me—oh, if only that were possible—to have them see what I'll see. I'll open my eyes so wide, so very wide, that the Parisians will be afraid. Yes, that's it, I'm going to scare them! In fact, I'm determined to scare them with my wide-open eyes. And I'll open all my pores, too, since I've got to take everything in! After all, Paris demands to be known, to be assimilated. I'll leave with the eyes of all my friends and relatives; I'll leave with their noses too so that we all can breathe the air of Paris, and with their feet so that all of us can tread Parisian soil—the Paris of the Three Musketeers, of Fanfan the Tulip, the Imperial Violets . . . the Paris of "Tchalé," Charlie Chaplin! Those days are long gone now, but the memories are as vivid as ever.

communal

I'm off to Paris! Can this really be happening? But under what title? I'm not famous. I'm neither a chief nor the president of an organization—not even one of those passive types who always does what is asked of them. I don't like concerts; I don't even like tailor-made clothes. And I certainly don't have a commission. Let's face it, I represent nothing. I have no assets propping me up, nor am I likely to have any in the future. And you and I both know this is an age when one is valued in terms of how much one has, how much one can raise and flaunt; in terms of how many people one can knock about, especially those tired and hungry masses, those scrawny, consumptive ones even Christ forgot to call up into the hills. I am one of those, one of the exhausted that God forgot to call—but one He'll call someday because it is the good and just thing to do. There's no doubt about it: we who are called last will, at that moment, be first. Who, then, will tell us He isn't fair? Those who were the first before and who, then as well as now, are still the first? Ever onward, never backward! A fine motto, a wonderful plan of action! Besides, didn't Christ forewarn us of this when He was forced to say, "Those who fall behind will find even their skin taken away"?

I'm still trying to figure it all out, but you, my friend, you for sure will understand why I go on and on about this ticket to Paris. Soon I can stop thinking about the Paris I've only seen on postcards or in films, the Paris others wanted me to see. I'll see what I want to see—the Châtelet prison if my heart is heavy with old memories, the Arch of Triumph if instead my heart's on fire. I'll be dependent upon no one. No one else's eyes will see for me, and no one else will think for me. I'm off on an adventure, and I'll be experiencing it for myself, for you, for all our people. I'm off—off to see Paris in the flesh, the Paris of living people, the Paris that talks and sings and dances and complains, the Paris that enjoys herself and yet takes time to reflect. I don't know what's happening inside me, but everything has changed, my friend, everything has changed since I decided to keep the ticket on me. I go to sleep thinking about Paris, and when I awake in the morning, I think I'm waking up in Paris. I'm here but I'm not here. Strange phenomenon. I look at people without seeing them; I hear what's being said but I don't absorb it. Paris has already captured me, just like our own genies do when they cast a spell over someone and remove their power of speech. Isn't that what's happening to me? I seem to be floating; I barely acknowledge anyone or anything. I tell you Paris must be a wicked city indeed; to be able to work that kind of magic from that great a distance means only one thing: the evil spirits there must definitely be stronger than ours, whom we abandon, and who in turn abandon us. Life is more than this. Like love, it's made up of the good turns we do for each other, the small attentions that give meaning to a friendship, the worries we share . . .

You must be wondering how I got the ticket. Well, I'll tell you. It was given to me! Can you believe it? One evening a white man and I were talking about Paris, about the whole idea of progress and all those problems that face us every day, and he said to me, "As you know, it's never easy to resolve differences of this magnitude, to help friends as much as one would like. Patience and understanding are needed on both sides, and much diplomacy. I fully understand your impatience, but when you walk down the Champs-Elysées and see the Paris that lies before you . . . By the way, have you seen the Champs-Elysées?"

"No."

"Then what did you see?"

"I've never been to Paris . . ."

"That's impossible! You've never been to Paris?"

"Never."

"Well, we'll see about that!"

Several days later, as he handed me the ticket I now carry around like a good-luck charm, he said, "My friend, here's your ticket to Paris."

From that moment on, those evil spirits of Paris have given me no rest. I feel lightheaded. All my worries have disappeared, and I find myself hopping about, whistling, singing . . .

I'm neither hungry nor thirsty. To tell the truth, I couldn't be happier! Paris! There must be nothing like it!

The plane [to Dakar] carried me off. Every time it dropped into an air pocket, I'd cling to my seat as if it were the only sure support to keep me from falling. The other passengers did the same. Man is an incredible idiot—he's always looking for support no matter how fragile it is. He's been walking so much since the world became world that he'd like nothing more than to rest, the sort of rest that's completely oblivious to a machine that only recently entered the race. We were like eggs inside a gigantic bird—and, given all those air pockets, no one knew where it would deposit us. You could say they were obstacles on the road to Paris. And they were so spiteful they'd wait until we were about to eat to make their appearance. You had the distinct feeling they wanted to test our "airborne" stomachs. Mine was for sure. In fact, very few of us could claim to be like birds, who can eat while flying and not get sick.

Dakar: I got up early to renew my acquaintance with the city. Automobiles rested all along the sidewalks, exhausted from their daily labors. Laundry hung from balconies and waved in the wind as if to arouse everything that passed by. In the street a cat stared at me—I wonder if it recognized me. A dog barked—it was clear he didn't know me at all. At this hour the whole world is still asleep, and I felt as though I had just disturbed the sleep of kings. With every step I took, memories came pouring forth and pressed around me. Every house, every post I leaned against, every tree had something to say to lead me back into the past. A new sound, however, had been added to those of times past: the sound of air conditioners. The Europeans were now bringing with them not only their customs but their climate as well. Alongside the more modern buildings—a sign of the future—stood several quaint little houses, one- or two-family dwellings with courtyards and gardens. As I listened to the sounds, I felt as though I were watching a capital city in evolution, a reflection of our own evolution, a generation with new ideas succeeding another in the same way the new buildings were replacing the old ones. Everything seemed to cry out "Progress! Progress!"

A houseboy was on his way to work; a car started off. Roosters doubled their efforts as if to say, "Arise, you men of little courage. Progress won't stand still for you. It awakens with the sun and goes to bed when it sets."

In Dakar you find newspapers of all persuasions. I was thumbing

home of a European influence

6

through *"L'Humanité"* and found myself remembering that unbelievable story of a search undertaken one morning in the streets of Treichville for two communists who used to come to the city on a regular basis. To organize such a frantic search for an idea is to give that idea an importance it may not have. And in our world of constant sun, search parties are forever organized to locate traffickers, border criminals, butterflies, and ideas. But no one ever really knows where they hide, for, as the proverb says, "Those who carry the drums aren't always the lead dancers." They have so many connections that it's sometimes difficult to exterminate them completely. I know it's hard for you to understand this, but no matter. What's important is to admit this sort of thing exists, even if we don't fully understand. Sometimes we even think we can stop a dance simply by grabbing hold of the one carrying the drum. What do we do, then, with the song running through peoples' heads? Can we stop it merely by saying, "Hey, you there! Leave at once!"? We can talk all we want to about head washing and brainwashing, but whether the head is black or white, blond or brunette—or even bald—we can never eliminate the song entirely.

political revolt

I think we're guilty of another transgression as well. Are we really living under a regime that values free thought? Is a human being as respected as he should be? Aren't we, instead, trying to make him into a robot? A parrot? A mannequin? Aren't we trying to remove what truly gives meaning to life—the right to believe what you want? After all, God gave man a head to think with—even the ability to express himself, for he was also given a mouth through which his own thoughts can be voiced. Where, then, are freedom and tolerance when people are forced to think alike? To pray and dance alike? And worse yet, to dream the same dreams? Fortunately, our differences remain, and we must always try to tune into what the person speaking to us is saying.

I watched the passersby, enigmas all of them, some smiling, others more serious. Each one moved in his own orbit, all the while talking of brotherhood.

At this point, the buildings increased in number, and Dakar spread out. The streets seemed dirty and much narrower but far more animated. There were many bookstores frequented by Africans—not as many as there should be, however, given a people on the verge of self-realization, a people about ready to reclaim their God-given rights.

Some faces I could attach names to. They kept saying I hadn't changed, that I was still "Blessed Bertin on the move."[1] "Twenty years have passed, and you have the same smile you had in 1936." I think they were exaggerating. But I didn't dare tell them so, for I was happy I hadn't changed, that I hadn't become someone else—happy too that I could knock a hole in the old saying "He who doesn't move forward falls behind." As far as I'm concerned, I've neither advanced nor retreated. A chrysalis? A cyst? I don't know. But my friends would say the same thing again one day.

Before me stood the administration building—a veritable beehive of activity. People were sweeping in and out of elevators. Motors hummed. At each floor, a wave of humanity. Those machines, however, rested heavily on the shoulders of those still on the ground floor. Occasionally a shutter opened. A window on the world, but a rearview window. Eyes were fixed on the door, as if ready to leave, to rush out before the boat sank. No one seemed to want to settle in there, to stay put and endure; rather, they preferred to remain on the fringe, looking, listening, observing with other eyes and ears that lay scattered around the city . . .

You wonder what kind of world we'd be living in if we were forced to marry mirror images of ourselves instead of distinctly unique personalities, if, to our friends, we looked and walked the same, thought and lied the same. I can promise you those friends would no longer believe in the one phrase that has saved us for centuries, that has drawn us to each other: "I'm not like anyone else." It's true. No two of us are ever the same—we never have the same sore spots, the same looks or smell.

What evil spirit makes me a prisoner of my own words just when I'm bound for Paris? To rid myself of these thoughts, I left for the offices of the Grand Council.

At the moment, the Grand Council isn't housed in a large mansion. If the council members inhabited fancy quarters simply because their wisdom teeth had appeared, we'd have to wait for them to pass the teething stage before the quarters fit them properly.

A beautifully decorated room with chairs, armchairs, and tables. Much commotion but a few empty places—those absent. Flags—

1. Tanhoé Bertin is Dadié's persona. For the Baoulé people of the Ivory Coast, the Tanhoé River is both the god of war and the guardian of religion. He is considered the enemy of all white people. See M. Battestini, S. Battestini, and Roger Mercier, *Bernard Dadié* (Paris: Fernand Nathan, 1964), 54. Dadié, of course, is indulging in a bit of irony here.

numerous flags for such a small place. On the wall a portrait of the president of the Republic on parade and others of governors-general now dead or still alive. An alliance of the dead and the living—doesn't that explain the strength of the city? There they are, watching over the debates, dictating to each his duty, a quaver in their voices, a welcome show of passion against a fatal opposition to progress, against predetermined attitudes . . . Photographers. And journalists who carry at the ends of their pens either the viper's venom or the bee's honey. Everyone was so caught up in what they were doing that many policemen stood guard.

To say yes, they lift a finger, the index finger, and the president counts those fingers, which speak for the people. And to say no, again the index finger is pointed upward, and the president counts those high-pitched voices also. You wonder where they acquired the detestable habit of not saying yes or no with their mouths. But maybe God knew all along they talked too much! It seems the whites do the same thing when they're in session. They talk, even argue; but when it comes time to vote, they pass their power of speech to their finger, which in turn becomes their mouthpiece and is considered such. Often the two sides will discuss for hours whether to put a comma at the end of a phrase or that chameleon of a mark—the semicolon. The French language is so precise, so very profound, that you can never take too many precautions. And those august presences who watch the proceedings rejoice when they see each disciple toe the mark and stay on track—as if they had a race to run. The two sides do quarrel, but just when you think they're going to throw themselves at each other and tear one another to bits, there they are, bursting with laughter. Having moved beyond the impasse, the discussion will take off again, but in another direction. And it will continue that way unless the president uses the powers the laws give him to cut off the debate and get things back on an even keel.

The issue is occasionally so specious that you never can quite get ahold of it, wring it dry, and have done. Such battles are exhausting; tempers flare up and harden despite the soft purring of the ventilators. The president will then call for a recess so that, in the corridors near the lobby area, an agreement can be worked out through favors and concessions on both sides.

A member of the Grand Council has reason to be important. He has the same needs we have, but the more important he is the more pronounced they are. The president will go so far as to adjourn the assembly in order to get his strength back. Here they say "to restore one's forces," and the phrase fits perfectly.

I felt myself in a world where things move slowly, like a river. I've had to reduce my speed a bit because there are so many twists and turns; as a result, I'm not yet at the end of my difficulties. To see Paris one needed more than a ticket. I was beginning to understand that if Paris surely deserved a mass in her honor because she wasn't built in a day, the same was even truer now, for it was impossible to even get there in forty-eight hours. They thought I would become discouraged when they forced me to run from one agency to another, when they threw obstacle after obstacle in my way and sent me from this person to that one. How many doors heard me knock? How many guards—one eye open, the other closed—called me back to show me the sign posted above them? I thought I could fool them. Alas, they were alert to such tricks. But I held firm and kept myself from saying, "Listen, I'm on my way to Paris." I know these types. They would have simply looked at me crosswise, shrugged their shoulders, and smirked. And I've never been able to get used to that sort of smile. They would never know that I had a good-luck charm in my pocket and that as long as it was there I would overcome all my problems, even if they were the size of mountains. Ah, it's not so easy to discourage a man who has a ticket for Paris in his pocket!

There was not one seat available on any airline, French or otherwise. They told me to take a boat. What else will they sing me to sleep with? "It's July"—as if I didn't know. "Teachers are returning home." What next? "It's the usual seasonal migration of all those who want to escape to a better climate." But they have nothing in common with me. And then, the supreme argument: "The president of the Republic has invited numerous people to celebrate July 14, and they have priority." Each explanation left me cold. All I knew was that I had a ticket to Paris, and because I did they had to get me there.

"I understand, but you don't have an official title . . . "

"I'm an administrative clerk, sir . . . "

"That's not sufficient . . . "

"But excuse me, sir, a government clerk, second class, third level, fourth step . . . "

"None of that matters."

All those titles I spent twenty years acquiring, that I thought I could use one day as a way in, as an "Open, Sesame!"—none of them counted. You've got to admit such people will drive you to despair.

"As I was saying, you're not one of those the president has invited. For those distinguished personalities we've got our orders: express service."

And so it was. He ended by throwing that in my face. I'm not among the distinguished. I kept insisting—perhaps a bit too much—that it wasn't my fault, but name one person in the same situation who would not have insisted! I'm nothing special—eh?

"Look here, maybe . . . "

The genies were no longer there to ply their magic and make someone special in a moment's notice. I understood: I was like a blank sheet of paper, without depth, without any distinguishing feature.

"Even a small seat will do."

"Everything is booked up through the end of the month."

This last comment went in one ear and out the other. I didn't want to keep it inside since I knew it would devastate me. Two weeks in Dakar. Okay, then, I'll agree to this, but only if I'm sure of a place then.

My deep sigh must have touched something inside them, especially in the young blond woman who had been listening without saying a word. Perhaps she thought someone was waiting for me in Paris, and each of us knows what it's like to wait. She looked at me sweetly, and her smile seemed to promise a seat on a plane bound for Paris. They thumbed through their papers. One, two, three . . . their heads came together. Their fingers came to a stop on my name—my heart. Finally, she raised her head; I looked at her.

"You may be in luck. The gentleman will check. Tell me, Maurice, has Mr. Paul confirmed his reservation yet?"

"Not yet."

"We could give his seat to this man."

"Yes."

"We'll sign you up, sir. Are you alone?"

"Yes, I'm alone! There's just one of me, just one!"

How many times I've said that I'll never know, but my every heartbeat has sung it also—alone! Alone! What can I tell you? Those evil spirits of Paris must be with me: there I am, one of the chosen, on the roll, my name inscribed, laid to rest on the passenger list. Everything in place. I'm swimming—beaming—with joy. I'm sinking, but instead of drowning I find myself breathing easier. I attend to what is going on around me—I'm in tune, I have a place. I see a ship entering port. I see the women struggling to keep their heavy breasts thrust forward, weighed down as they are with the stares of men. The heat seems here to stay, like one of those European permanent waves. Bets are waged on how long it will last, and we are the ones who always suffer in the end. I must now learn how to run in order to be in tune with my arrival. I'm told that what the Parisians admire most is one's tone, the right pitch, which, in any situation, is considered "la." How can I possibly learn how to run in a country where no one is in a hurry? Can't you guess what they'll call me? Why they'll think I'm crazy! How many problems we encounter in life! How difficult it is even to follow along, not to mention keep up! Even though you're constantly on the alert, you almost never know what key you're in because you're always trying to figure it out. Too bad. Let them think what they will; I'll learn how to run. And speaking of that, how do you run in Paris? Do you take small steps? Long strides? Do you run in twos? Everyone will tell you that in order to truly become a part of Paris, to clothe yourself in her two thousand years of history in only several months, you need to run. "Oh yes, to be sure, over there people run. They're always running." But they never tell you how those strange Parisians manage to run without getting winded. As for me, I'm already exhausted, and I haven't even reached my destination. No, it's just not possible that an entire people spends its time running. And there's no one to say to them, "Enough of this running. Let's stop a moment and wait for the others." We always do this when we set out from one village for another. We'll stop to tell a funny story or two, to sing a bit, even to take a nap at the foot of a large tree near a stream. Eat, walk, work, sing, dance, sleep—that's what we do. But run? Why? What for?

It seems too that people there don't even consider this, partly because the streets are so different. All along those huge boulevards they all keep to themselves, even though they move at the same pace as the others. All push their own plow, follow their own furrow, carry their own load of hopes and dreams. . . . And those dreams lighten their burden and give them wings—just as mine have done ever since I was given a ticket to Paris.

I'm now at <u>Yoff.</u> The formalities taken care of, I make my way down a noisy hallway. Since I know none of the people whose paths I cross, I feel very much alone. Before, when two blacks would meet they'd stop and greet each other, they'd ask for the news from home, they'd ask about their families. Now they all go their own way without even so much as a smile. Everyone's geared up, and the whites want out. It's curious, but I no longer feel rushed; there is in me that sense of calm which often precedes important events. I'm not even worried anymore.

I make my way almost unconsciously while planes keep landing and taking off. Finally it's our turn. "Those passengers departing for Paris"—I'd been waiting for this to be announced. People watched us as we were hurried toward the boarding area. Yes, gentlemen, I too am on my way to Paris. I too count for something. I'm the only black among all those white passengers. I take a window seat. No one wants to sit next to me. They all notice the empty seat beside me, but they all pass on by. Habit tells them to sit next to someone of their own color. I can understand this since I've often done the same thing, but this time I realize just how much color separates people. It must have taken enormous courage for this one passenger to become my neighbor. We do not speak, but we're neighbors just the same.

*
* *

Here we are, both sensible people, both comfortably settled in our seats, our beds; two different worlds side by side in a machine that could reduce us to nothing at any moment. Only our cries of pain, our last gasps would prove that we are the same despite our differences, despite the color barrier. The lights are turned off. How are you supposed to sleep when you're between heaven and earth? The towns file by; you recognize them by their numerous bright lights. A lighthouse approaches, blinks a salute, then moves off into the distance. Where are we? I take my shoes off in order to be more comfortable. Have I been asleep? Is it still daytime? What's going on? It's four o'clock, and you'd think it's six in the morning. My watch must have stopped. My seatmate's says the same thing. Something's out of whack. Is the sun getting up too early? Yes, it's daytime for sure. What sort of country am I heading for anyway? One where day begins at four o'clock? I'm beginning to understand why people there must run; they don't want the sun to beat them in the race through the day. They want to be able to flee with the day when night approaches.

And what do they serve us with breakfast? Forms to fill out. No one can travel without the state knowing about it. A police state takes these airplanes and transforms them into branches of their intelligence network. The clouds are as white as cotton and so bright that you can't look at them. We're sailing on an ocean of clouds, our gigantic flying machine swaying over its waves.

My shoes are no longer where I put them. How can I find them without getting up, especially here, where we all stay put right where we are, and barely speak to our neighbors? Here where the people have no fire in their hearts nor in their arms but only in their legs? Whites are not rich when it comes to words. Is that because words have a way of taking off in their own direction, of assuming a different meaning as soon as they leave the threshold of one's mouth? I manage to find my shoes, but it's impossible to get them on. Have my feet grown? I stare at them; I try rubbing them. There's a good chance I'll land in Paris barefooted! And that's not the best way to present yourself to the Parisians. Oh no, either they'll go on of their own free will, or I'll force them on—one way or another, my shoes will do what they were designed to do. Lacking a shoehorn, I do battle with a pencil; unfortunately, it breaks. But that's better than arriving in Paris barefooted. Below us farmland extends for miles. The fields are all carefully outlined and in order—all beautifully maintained, each one a different color. People here must dye their land; otherwise, how could they give it so many wonderfully different colors—everything from reddish yellow to dark green? Roads too of all sorts and towns, one after the other. Not one piece of ground goes to waste. For sure this land must be ruled by a people who toe the mark, a square and chalk-line in their minds and eyes. Phenomenal creatures, these people; they're all in love with the perfectly straight line, one without even the slightest smudge. It looks as though they even prune their weeds. And yet, they claim they never have time for that. Over there, a castle surrounded by trees; over here, a factory; and, as far as the eye can see, the same landscape of roads and carefully marked fields. The way they work the ground shows just how much these people don't know when it comes to understanding what life really means. For them, life must follow its usual course, everything in its proper channel, everything tractable and conforming to their own desires—everything, in sum, like perfectly trimmed nails. Get off the beaten path—that's what I say. They're an old people with old habits, but life stays young only if you're thrown off course now and then. Propped up by centuries of civilization, they'd love to see it bow down before them, but life continues to mock them. It witnessed the building of the pyramids, which even today are still being explored. Yes, they'd love to preserve it—in tins perhaps—but life is forever laughing in their faces. That drives them to despair, and they're constantly tearing their hair because of it. That's why so many white people are bald. And once their hair has fallen out, life can further torment them by polishing those sore spots every morning: that also explains the shine on the backs of their heads.

We can see people below us now. My neighbor and I bid each other good day, and the stewardess smiles at me as she takes our declaration forms. The atmosphere changes; masks come off, and people become their old selves again. Paris is draped in fog, her face hidden from me. And I, who had dreamed of flying over her, who had wanted to embrace her in a single glance and shout to all who could hear, "Paris, you're more magnificent than all other cities put together!" saw only the airport—Orly. first disappointment

THE FIRST THING handed me was *L'Air de Paris*. I admire this way of welcoming visitors, of putting them in the mood and alerting them to the city's customs, its ticks. *L'Air de Paris!* Armed with this review, you'll keep from committing all sorts of blunders. Paris not only welcomes you in a painless way, she also offers you her views on life. What's more, this brochure is given to all visitors, even to whites. The city figures that even if you're gone for only two weeks, you can lose your footing by the time you return. That, I must say, is truly Parisian.

I'm in Paris; I tread its ground. Everywhere I look, I see white people; white workers. Not a black face anywhere. There's no doubt about it, this is a country of white people. It's cold; the sun, feeling ashamed, has gone into hiding. It's aware of having committed an injustice toward me by burning me black from head to toe and barely even tanning the people here. Cars whiz by they're going so fast, but not the sound of a single horn. Honking is forbidden. Everyone obeys this rule. Where I'm from, it's also forbidden, but everyone delights in breaking the rule; in fact, they love to honk. It puts you in the limelight; it makes you "someone." Here taxi-drivers signal when they stop or start off. Goodness knows how long they've done this! But what goes on here is completely different from what happens back home. There, because taxi-drivers consider everyone they pass a potential customer, they steer with one finger always pointing up. If someone on the sidewalk nods, they skid to a halt, tires screeching. Too bad for the person behind them. But that's the code of the "jungle." There are flowers everywhere and cars parked all over the place. Posters and advertisements on the walls. I pay for a seat on the bus heading for the Invalides. Money takes on meaning again. The words "gratis" and "free of charge" surely must not exist in the vocabulary here. You're forever reaching into your pocket, forever figuring out how much something costs. What a country!

The first person I see is an old man on crutches talking to a friend, next, a factory worker on a bicycle, and then two children. Activity increases the closer you get to the city: people everywhere—in the streets, in cafes and restaurants. If I were home, I'd think this was a holiday. Traffic and more traffic, but it moves in an orderly fashion.

Cars stop at red lights and wait patiently for them to change to green before starting off again. Constant movement. The pedestrians seem the most pressed; after all, there're more of them. You should see them weave in and out of traffic and then, all of a sudden, stop. They must attach springs to their legs every morning.

You'd think the gray walls and buildings would have an effect on their dispositions. Wrong! They've got humor to spare. And to think they're also surrounded by continuous noise. Why the Parisians would think the world had stopped turning if, one morning, they didn't hear those familiar sounds. They're also a people who constantly look at their watches. But theirs is a city that captures you and sweeps you off despite yourself, and you're forced to adopt her pace whether you want to or not. Here there's no pulling back; you've got to keep going, keep moving to survive. You also notice that the electric lights are kept on during the day in restaurants and stores—probably so you can see your bill clearly. I'll never be afraid of going over the same ground twice here, for in this city you always have the feeling you're going in circles. You always seem to end up in the same district, with the same people, the same white faces. Here the raincoats we wear at home only when it rains are an integral part of one's dress. Given the houses piled one atop the other and the numerous streets that never intersect at right angles, Paris is a city that can't be harnessed. You feel that right off; it's what you notice first. And even if you were to put chains on the people, they'd somehow manage to get out of them; they're like fish before bait—they'd tear it to pieces in order to escape. That's imprinted in the very nature of the Parisian; it's embedded in his every attitude. Parisians enjoy their freedom. This is their city, and they know it. And to be a part of all this is irresistible.

The houses here are so serious-looking you'd think they're aware of what they are, of what they represent. They belong to Paris. Indeed, they are Paris.

*
*   *

Here, every person, every thing projects a certain air even though it tries not to show it.

Today is July 14, the most celebrated of Parisian holidays. It commemorates the capture of a prison named the Bastille. If the people are of one mind when it comes to celebrating this event, they aren't so when it comes to telling how something happened in the time of their ancestors. There are so many different versions that you no longer know who or what to believe. And since they are Parisians, and since all Parisians love to recount their history, you must give the impression they're each telling the truth. Being a good listener is, of course, considered polite here. However, they all attest to the fact that their history is not only long and involved but also filled with many rat- and toad-infested prisons.

As to the actual fall of the Bastille, some say the people who marched that day were bent on destroying an edifice that had, for four hundred years, represented absolute royal power. Since they had seen the face of the Bastille more often than that of the king, they hated him with a passion. And there's some truth to this. With no communication whatsoever between the classes, a rift was bound to grow. The king had put the Bastille between himself and the people, and the people would never forgive him. Others, on the contrary, believe the event happened by chance, that it was not deliberately planned. The people were looking for weapons; they met at the Bastille; the Bastille simply fell into their hands. Those in control had been frightened by the power of the masses before them and had sought refuge in their homes for a time. So many versions, so many contradictions only serve to restore my own self-confidence. It proves that despite what is written in textbooks, memory has its limits. More than anything else, it shows that each of us sees the past in our own particular way given our own particular upbringing. And that's why four people describing one event will give you four different versions. Even here. The Parisians are no different from anyone else. One thing is clear, however: the Bastille was taken. On this point they all agree, so much so, in fact, that they'll swear to it. And ever since, on July 14, the Parisians celebrate anew their hard-won freedom. Forever wanting to serve as examples, they love for others to take part in the festivities; they want others to know that they too had once been subjugated, that by sheer patience, hard work, and determination, they had won back their self-respect. They want people everywhere to remember that it was the Parisian who reintroduced the idea of individual freedom and respect for the common person. And with good reason. After all, a Bastille is not taken every day. Yes, as I've said, it's July 14. But there are few flags to be seen. Government buildings have put them up; the streets, boulevards, and department stores, however, have kept their usual look. Without flags. Against such restraint, our sprawling displays seem scandalous.

Why we alone have more flags than five million Parisians do. To show our patriotism we put flags in our windows. In fact, we put them everywhere—in the streets and railroad stations, on trees, government buildings, businesses, private residences, canoes, taxis, people . . . At times, our women even make jackets out of flags. To show just how much Paris is a part of them, they wear on their bodies what they feel in their hearts. But then, am I not in a country where love involves quiet moments, soft whisperings, and shy glances? I don't think the Parisian woman would let herself be caught dressed like that. Therefore, only God knows whether she truly loves her city. Here flags are only used to drape the coffins of famous men; we, on the other hand, are neither dead nor famous. But madness does have its limits. And yet, won't a woman go to any lengths to show her love for a husband who's a bit reticent when it comes to exhibiting his feelings? If husbands are polygamous, it's because their wives love them more when they have to compete openly for their affection.

Parisians may be stingy when it comes to parading their flag openly, but they carry it in their hearts like a precious jewel; and when they die, a bit of the flag dies with them. It's the only love that proves forever true, and they live and die for it. Since they know the value of their emblem, they don't like to carry it over their arms. They only brandish it in the faces of their enemies, and then with the intent to beat their brains out with it. You can take away everything they have, they can surrender it all, but they'll never give up their flag, their history, their identity. And yet, whenever they talk about the flag, it's always in such a joking way that you'd think it means nothing to them. Wrong, my friend! It's the nature of the Parisians to talk about serious things in a lighthearted way. It's so much a part of their manner that when a catastrophe occurs—let's say, a house collapses on its inhabitants— newspapers will treat it as a mere incident. I have a suspicion Parisians pay more attention to things rather than people and would prefer to risk damaging their hearts than to lose the appearance of being in control.

The traditional review of the troops. No blubber-pots here, but no beauty contestants either. The one who works the hardest this day is the chief of state. He must decorate and kiss all those good soldiers who guarded every inch of the country's borders; he must chat with them and shake their hands. All of this he must do with a smile—even if he has a migraine—it's all part of his role as arbiter.

And these people who worship their *café-filtre*—that elegant way of passing time, of lingering with a sweetheart who otherwise might weigh anchor and take off—have as ancestors the Visigoths, the Germans, the Burgundians, Goths, and Franks, who, driven by hunger and the search for adventure, came from all over. The newcomers proceeded to set up housekeeping with the Gauls, who had already established residence. I'm not quite sure how this worked; it happened so long ago that no one remembers the details. But it seems that all these tribes were absorbed into the Gallic melting pot, and out of this came the Franks, whose descendants are best represented by the Parisians. I'm still trying to understand all this. Apparently the Gauls who resided in Paris were farmers and boatmen. They formed themselves into a corporation of sailors and adopted as their emblem a sailing ship and the motto *Fluctuat nec mergitur*[1] as a way of mocking the Romans—those other conquerors who had thought they could change the Gallic way of life. The Romans had wanted to make all the Parisian boatmen farmers. No greater blow could have been given to the Parisians and their burgeoning pride. And for centuries Paris kept yelling that it wasn't a final resting place. But people didn't listen; in fact, they even saw the motto as an invitation. Beautiful, old, filled with witty, flirtatious women, and brimming with flowers and light—this city, this Paris has everything to draw the adventurer. The Romans did manage, though, to leave their mark—in the form of arenas, cemeteries, and most probably a descendant or two.

You keep wondering what would have become of Paris if Clovis—whose name means "illustrious warrior"—had not made the city his capital the day after he had suffered a defeat. Indeed, you could say Paris was born from a defeat. This Clovis went on to become a saint. I wonder if he suffered a defeat expressly so that he could then serve a god who wanted to make Paris what it is today. No one has been able to explain this to me. His wife Clotilde—an illustrious warrior in her own right—is also a saint. For both husband and wife to be saints is increasingly rare nowadays, because men and women—even those who are married—no longer think in the same way; they no longer have the same tastes or wish for the same things.

If a marriage is teetering on the brink, the heart should intervene. It should tell the head not to take the final plunge and warn the imagination not to stray too far afield—after all, the living room is territory

1. See page 131 for a full discussion. Paris's motto means "It is tossed by the waves but does not go under."

enough for whatever fantasies one has ... With all its warrior-saints, you're inclined to think that Paris is partial to warriors. But enough! We could go on with this forever!

If Paris is so civilized, so adored by the gods, it's because it had as its godmother Queen Clotilde and, as its patron saint, Geneviève, "Daughter of Heaven." On the advice of these two women, Clovis, the king, asked that a basilica be built in honor of Saints Peter and Paul on the top of a hill named Saint Geneviève. Saint Peter had in his possession the keys to paradise, and no one could enter without his permission. When he died, he left his successor not only the keys but his crown as well. Adjoining the keys to paradise were the keys to hell, a place where the souls of those who had sinned were kept burning. While alive, they had not followed the laws of God or, more precisely, had not interpreted them as they should have been interpreted. Their God was not at all fatherly. We, on the other hand, brought our god down to our own level; we gave him wives and children whom even Spider likes to trick. He regards us as his children and we treat him like a father. We trust each other. We might neglect him sometimes, but we always seek his help whenever something goes wrong. We always say that he is just above our heads. The people here, however, don't even know where to find their God, despite the fact that, like us, they place him just above their heads. This is tantamount to saying that we're both in the dark, or they're not telling the truth. Since they adore myths and fairy tales, they always give their heroes supernatural origins. The natural ones are too simple and, therefore, unsuitable for those whom they consider great and glorious. They maintain, for instance, that the great-great-grandfather of Clovis was a sea monster. It seems you can be a true Parisian and still reason like an Agni.[2]

But I suppose that's what draws us to these people, what makes them fascinating. I've even discovered that many of their folktales are similar to ours. Even if mothers here push their babies around in what look like tiny beds on wheels, even if they choose not to breastfeed, they still love their children. And whenever I see a father holding his son by the hand, happily telling him stories, I say to myself, "Why, they're acting like black people." Yes, in many ways they're like us; they also love children. What, on the other hand, they find abhorrent is a young mother who doesn't have an official husband. They want her to have a

2. The Agni are a tribe located primarily in the region between the Volta River (Ghana) and the Bandama River (Ivory Coast).

title since it's titles they respect most. How can I explain these titles? Here you find a number of words that can't be translated into any other language. For example, it's possible to have an official wife—assuming such a title existed—one who would fill the role of a real wife; you can be a governor or an acting governor; you can even be called salesman, as you are. To make this clearer, whenever you ask people for their official title, it's best if they answer directly and convincingly with "I'm a businessman" or "I'm a farmer" or "I'm such and such." The title becomes a reference point, and once you know it, you'll be in tune with the person you're speaking with. It's all a matter of getting the right pigeonhole, the right drawer or index file. If you're a farmer, you'll be asked right off—in the name of pure information—what you grow. The conversation, thus focused, will have a better chance of staying on track. If you're lucky, the person might also pull out his second memory—the one he keeps in his pocket—and take down your address. And yet, when all is said and done, is anything in life certain? Do we ever really know anything? The good-natured Parisian, seemingly without a care in the world, is always thinking about tomorrow, always doing everything he can to assure himself a bright future. But plan ahead as he may, he only takes himself into consideration.

Besides, the French language is so difficult that I'm often asking myself if they themselves always understand what is being said. This reminds me of a delightful mishap I once had. A department head asked me one day to assemble the papers he had set aside for me. I grabbed the stapler and—*tac!* Pleased with having done this so quickly, I proudly presented myself before him.

"But I told you to assemble them."

"That's what I did."

"Assemble them in the sense of gathering them up, of putting them together with those that are still scattered about."

Ever since then, I've distrusted myself when it comes to speaking this language. Moreover, I've come to the conclusion that all the different nuances we can attach to a word result not only in countless misunderstandings but also explain many of our daily traumas. Anyway, to get back to the point, having a baby without being married is seen as something bad. The child may be a child, and that's good, but it won't be a good child—do you follow? Let me assure you, they're always splitting hairs, always twisting something around to suit them. But I understand why. In a country where any number of ways are available to help you avoid such "errors," if instead you choose to go your own

labels

way, you're—as they say—not on top of things, not in tune with others, not on the same level. And the Parisians don't like that. They don't like for someone to lag behind. After all, aren't they the brains of the world? And if the brains fail, what will happen to the feet? That's what's meant by the phrase, "Paris, the city of light."

I haven't seen a statue of Saint Geneviève anywhere. They must hide their patroness. For centuries now she's patiently watched over the city; she knows the magic that Paris continues to work on people, especially those who, despairing of ever having such a city, prefer instead to come and pillage—as that first-class barbarian Attila did. They say that everywhere his horse stepped, the grass refuses to grow. I think he was given the name "Scourge of God." This conqueror marched through Paris. The frightened inhabitants fled. Geneviève halted the exodus, raised an army, supplied the city with necessary provisions, and restored courage to those who had lost it when they were overtaken by fear. She was the soul of the resistance movement. And, as you know, when a woman puts up resistance, there's only one thing to do: attack. This is exactly what that wise Scourge of God did: he must have known all about women who resist. Geneviève had promised the Parisians help from above, and that help came when Attila was defeated on the Catalonian Plain as he was retreating with his troops. Immediately after performing these miracles, Geneviève was made a saint; that is, she became one of the dead who sees, hears, and lives in the company of God.

But what Paris hated more than anything else was "the Norman Affair." This was a long drawn-out feud without any clear direction whatsoever. There they were one morning: Normans in boats right at the city gates. The Normans must have truly resented the Parisians, for they were primed and ready to do battle. Saint Geneviève was forced to summon Saint Germain for help in booting out those Norman devils. No one remembers anymore which Germain it was, Des Près or Auxerrois. Memories simply don't agree on this point. But it really doesn't matter; the important thing is that they were able to annihilate the Normans by pouring boiling oil and tar on them. The Parisians had sensed the fact that the Normans would not take kindly to the idea of donating additional monies, in the form of mandatory taxation or otherwise, for the honor and glory of Paris.

Parisians have never forgotten this. Hence, when they say they're speaking like a Norman, what they mean is "saying no without actually saying so," or "saying yes but really meaning no," or worse yet, "saying yes but meaning neither yes or no." That's what's meant by "the implied yes." Wouldn't you agree that the Parisians are now doing battle with the Normans on the latter's own terms? You also hear it said that the Normans—as good Normans would, remembering their struggle of long ago—don't want anyone to provoke them into a "Parisian Affair" (an expression not yet found in the dictionary because at present there are many more Parisians among the ranks of the immortals). But the Normans, with their customary patience, await their time, their own hour of glory.

For the moment, though, Paris is celebrating July 14. Accustomed to playing different roles, to dividing their time between work and play, the Parisians have turned over their voices this evening to the public squares, most especially to the Place de la Concorde, which, considering how brightly lit up it is, must be the most cherished place of all. She points to the heavens her finger-like Obelisk, and she is joined in her gaze by the statues encircling her; they all seem to have joined together to give who knows what advice to the various and sundry tourists, married couples, and friends on the verge of letting themselves go. But except for the young lovers lost in their own dreamworld, do any of them understand? You'd think you were in broad daylight; the crowds are so thick, the commotion so great, that if a rock were thrown into the air, it would never reach the ground. Cars press against each other with their bumpers and spin around in all directions as if blinded by the light. Every car from every avenue in Paris is here. No one could convince me that there was any other vehicle on any other street anywhere. Fireworks stream upward, taking with them the stares of thousands. Fountains flow freely, and the sound of falling water drowns out the noise of the metro crowds. An immense French flag, its three colors all made of fireworks, shoots out from the Arch of Triumph and seems, for a brief moment, to blanket Paris before it disappears into the clouds. The dead are part of the celebration too, and Paris, in full splendor, illuminates the skies with the symbol of freedom. The city seems to be playing dress-up with the lights, draping some over itself, sprinkling others on its hair and face. It is, then, a gray city only during the day. The miracle takes place at night, when it becomes a mass of sparkling white lights—lights that wink at you, beckon you, follow you around and detain you, then grab you by the nose and lead you to a shop window. The only thing you don't pay for here is the right to look, to browse. And Paris does all it can to make you admire its shop windows. After all, the city creates what it does, dreams and thinks what it wills, not to give us new needs but to raise us above the ordinary and everyday, to invite us to dream, to see life as a poem—rhythmic, sensuous, radiant.

The benches are filled with lovers locked in embrace, with spectators tired of standing up. Photographers rush up to take your picture, then give you their address. Paris is a city that has reversed the order of things: it awakens only after dark. The streets and avenues and boulevards, the lights—everything comes alive only at night. Pedestrians are so sure of themselves that motorists, doubting not only their rights but even what's on their right, stop and let them pass. No, here you haven't time to hesitate; you've got to keep going, whether you're crossing a street, catching a bus or a subway train, simply asking for information, or trying to get a woman's attention. The last won't always acknowledge you, especially if she's trying not to lose sight of a dream hovering overhead. It's much easier to get information in the metro, and I've come to understand why many a love is born there. As you look at the subway map, pretend you're lost and trying to find the right station. Head off in the wrong direction at least three times; after all, you never manage to get things right the first time in this spiderweb of color. Just when you think you're not following the right tone, when you feel you're about to plant roots there, get out the tuning fork—that is, step back and look at the map once again. Nod your head to convince yourself that you haven't moved your thumb, and then, as resolutely as possible, even if you're sure you're going to get lost, take off in the direction your eyes light on first. But here's the important part: swallow what pride you have and ask the person who's waiting to punch your ticket, "Excuse me, but to get to...Pigalle...?" Man or woman, they'll be sure to smile at you. But keep a tight grip on your pride and wait for their answer. It's sure to come after the smile: "Take Charenton des Écoles and then change at Madeleine." This isn't necessarily the shortest route, but it's probably the easiest. A moment ago, I said something about tone. To make sure you're still following the right color code, simply look at the people around you. They may not say anything, but their eyes will stay focused on you and your finger. As soon as you're about to leave, two or three of them will mouth a quiet "thank you," which means "It's high time; we were about to lose patience." If, by chance, you get off key, don't worry too much; just take off once again. I guarantee that everything will come together in one grand song in the end. I truly believe it's the songwriters who direct this city and the movement of its countless tourists, who conduct the song and laughter and dance that is Paris. This is difficult to explain; you must be a part of it to understand. The kings didn't understand the Parisians' love of life and ended up losing not only their crowns but also their heads in the Place de la Concorde. It's a place to be revered, a historical place where you should walk in silence as you listen for the murmurings and sighs of those who were here in times past, as you try to imagine the fears of some and the joys of others, as you try to encompass it all—the dreams, the cries and tears and whimperings of those on the death barrows. Here hopes were born and allowed to blossom; here too dreams were lost. Paris freed its people from crown rule and put its kings on the level of ordinary citizens. Yes, Place de la Concorde represents those heroic times, and it's called "Concorde" not only because the Parisians love brotherhood and peace but also because they tend to believe in the significance of names.

In the beginning, the Parisians supported their kings. As time went on, however, they began to feel the weight of that support. And when the level of misery and suffering kept rising, they glanced toward Saint Geneviève—as they were wont to do in such circumstances—and hoped for help from their protectoress, who, after all, was accustomed to rescuing them when trouble threatened. But since the kings were Parisians too Saint Geneviève found herself in an embarrassing situation, for she would have to intervene in a very delicate, in-house affair. Everyone kept saying, "If our Patron Saint says nothing, it means she consents to what's going on." Meanwhile, the kings held firm, and conditions remained the same. But the people kept hoping Saint Geneviève would intervene. With every passing year, the kings wanted more and more. And to support their bulging appetites, more and more money was needed. The kings may have worn the crown, but the people felt its weight. Their most famous king, the one called the "Sun King," shed his light over nearly four thousand courtiers, all of whom enjoyed themselves at the peoples' expense. Their duties included keeping the king company and knowing just what to say to him—that is, keeping him informed of what was happening but always from their own privileged point of view—and singing his praises far and wide. These courtiers were called nobles, a class of men bearing the names of their respective towns, rivers, mountain ranges, or places of origin. When they were born, their cradles came already equipped with a sword to show allegiance to their king, a castle and private fortune of their own, even their own personal crown. They went nowhere without their crown—just like our own tribal chiefs. This way the people could tell right off who they were—creatures always searching for a way to distinguish themselves. The nobles were divided and subdivided into such categories as those of ancient stock or lineage who had inherited the title, those who had acquired the title through armed service to the king, those who had been appointed courtiers, and those who enjoyed ducal or coronet status. All these men depended upon their divinely appointed king for their daily bread. The true God thus found Himself with two living representatives on earth. To avoid conflict, one was to take care of matters spiritual; the other, matters temporal. With such an apportionment, one forgot the ordinary citizen, who's made, it's said, in God's image and partakes of His Spirit. The poor, still languishing in sin, had only one role, to suffer, and only one duty, to pray; and to include in those prayers the king and his relatives, the friends of those relatives and even their families, all their castles, their pains and joys and dreams. Imagine, a god among mortals who was subject to the same weaknesses all humans are! Thus tormented, thus burdened, and despairing of help from their still-silent patron saint, the Parisians rolled up their sleeves and shouted, "God helps those who help themselves!" And if they are now so fiercely Cartesian, such good disciples of the philosopher Descartes, it's because people tried for so long to make them believe that the moon was made of green cheese, that babies came from storks, and that children gave birth to parents. After years of being tossed about and thrown in prison, even in the Bastille itself, they began to take action. People said it was only a temper tantrum, that it would pass. But to show they'd finally understood and were ready to fight back, the Parisians changed their money in secret. They got rid of their long woolen stockings.[3] What drove them to do this? What can you make of the fact that they were squirreling away their gold coins? Could you even find out if you asked? They looked across at the Bastille, which disfigured the landscape, robbed them of breath, and sent their dreams tumbling. There inside were people who had dared to criticize the monarchy. Lawyers had been retained, but despite their grand attempts to purge the judges' minds, they weren't always successful in extricating their clients from the Bastille's murky confines. Saint Geneviève continued to say nothing, as did all the other saints associated with the city. The king didn't understand what the people were grumbling about since their words reached him in terms suitable for his royal, indeed divine, ears. Their familiar

3. This refers to the change from breeches to long pants.

moorings gone, the two sides decided to meet. They talked for several days, but neither side understood what the other was saying. The king's representatives talked of money, and as far as the Parisian delegates were concerned, they might as well have been speaking a foreign language. The Parisians talked of individual rights, but what they said merely bounced off their listeners' ears. Fed up with the way things were going—and, for the moment, forgetting the Bastille—the king ordered the room evacuated. Then the unheard-of happened. One of the Parisian delegates stood up and shouted, "We're here by the will of the people. You'll have to force us out with bayonets!"

And thus it was uttered: the famous phrase that each generation teaches its young, the phrase that would topple kings and change the course of history.

They wanted bayonets; they got bayonets. Alas, these were as firm in their mission as the people were in theirs. The Parisians had but one thing in mind: the Bastille and the pain it caused. It stood dark and foreboding, a giant shadow on their sky and horizon. Events followed their natural course, and the battle between the people and the king finally reached its critical point. The saints remained silent. No one has been able to explain this terrifying silence. Perhaps God's official emissaries were themselves torn between the two camps. Who knows for sure, but the battle ended with the taking of the Bastille—that memorable event which is being celebrated with such ceremony today. With the capture of the Bastille, the people were freed of an enormous weight. Paris breathed again. Not long afterward, the king had his head chopped off. How very Christian of these Parisians, good churchgoers all! . . . From that day on, kings sat uneasy on thrones that had become very shaky indeed. Paris had proven to an astonished world that kings were mortal too. However, don't think for a minute that the Parisians are simple souls. They might love to stare dreamily at the Seine flowing by, but they are woven of many contradictions. After all, they're a blend of Goth and Visigoth, Alaman, Frank, and Parisian. Whether you approach them from the back or the front, the right or the left, it's one or the other of these temperaments you're seeing. That's why whatever judgments you make about them must be qualified. But it's easy to find fault with them since the side of them you see most often, the Frankish side, is the only one they want to show the world. And yet, these people who, if pushed far enough, lose patience and chop off the heads of kings, also love grass and trees and babbling brooks, and running barefooted through green fields. They adore vacationing in the country, among birds, lying down on the ground and watching the clouds roll by, and doing other silly, childish things. There they can commune with nature, drink in the sun and clean air. Moreover, they have an inordinate love of flowers and spend vast sums of money on them: what they don't give to beggars, they willingly give to anything that has to do with flowers. Maybe they belong to the flower caste, as some of us at home belong to the rain caste, the yam caste, or the parrot caste. We might scorn them back home, but here flowers are revered, even worshipped. Make no mistake about it, these people are truly strange. They show their love by sending flowers, and they never accept an invitation without bringing armfuls to their hostess. In fact, they take them everywhere. But I understand why, and so I forgive them. If, like us, they had forests all around them, they wouldn't give grass and trees and flowers such a prominent position in their lives. Here you can step on peoples' toes, but you'd better not step on a plot of grass. It's just not done. There're signs telling you not to; furthermore, if you do, everyone will give you dirty looks. Besides, the care they lavish on their parks and gardens goes to show just how important these landscapes are to people. Yes, the Parisians are definitely strange. They somehow manage to love, all at once, dogs, water, wind, grass, flowers, women, children, coffee, music, politics, Camembert cheese, and that most ignoble beast of all, that symbol of wickedness and treachery—the cat, and especially the black cat, master artist of deception.

THE PEOPLE HERE have also given each flower a particular meaning, which they study with great care.

And given their penchant for categorizing everything, they've even established a flower hierarchy. The flower they love best, the one whose smell intoxicates them the most and makes their eyes roll in utter ecstasy, is the rose, which to them means "May the love we share always be as strong." Who doesn't swoon at such a velvet-soft proposal, quivering with promise? There's no sight more beautiful than that of a woman smelling a flower. In fact, there's nothing more exciting than to watch her eyelids closing in rapt attention, her nostrils dilating and her bosom rising seductively as her breathing slows down. For sure it's no accident that Paris has so many flowers and flower shops. Why, the people even put flowers on windowsills, and the first thing they do when they get up in the morning is water them. They may forget to drink their coffee but never to water their flowers. The women themselves seem to be walking flowers as they move in and out of flower shops. Their passion for flowers has even entered their language, for they speak of a "flowery style." I'll wager they even cry when they see a rose lose its leaves. And to watch such a beautiful thing die and know that you're helpless to save it is sad indeed. At such times, thoughts turn invariably to our own destiny.

That special way of looking at roses, carnations, and other flowers also extends to women, who parade their own colors—the rouge on their lips and cheeks—in front of everyone. They want to remain forever, for men, the beautiful flowers they are now. Yes, they may have thorns, but what rose doesn't?

After centuries of firsthand experience, a man has learned to show so much respect for a woman that she manages somehow to always withdraw those thorns. He helps her sit down and get up; he takes off her coat and helps her put it back on; he opens the car door for her. She is treated like a queen. He's constantly telling her what she wants to hear—how beautiful she is, how charming and alluring. He talks of her irresistible smile and the golden light emanating from her eyes. He's forever trying to make the same old expressions sound new and appealing once more. And the woman believes him—that's the miraculous thing about language. It's as though she's hearing those words for the first time. The words may be old—that's for sure—but don't they sound new when someone else says them? A woman is so fine, so delicate, so much the precious flower, that man must approach her with caution. First, he brings his feet together; then, as he leans forward and moves into a slow bow, he seizes the hand the woman extends graciously and brings it to his lips. This is called "kissing" her hand. These men are hard to figure out; they may have done away with the court, but they've nonetheless adopted its manners. You've got to see this to realize just how much homage is given to a hand that can be affectionate one minute and scratch the next. But this is their way of getting a woman's attention, and of keeping it for a moment. Since they don't want a woman's head to turn away in fear that she hasn't succeeded in turning theirs, they give her a dose of well-spoken phrases. And just think—the women appear content as they listen to those fine words. After all, they don't hear them every day. But the day comes when many women have had their fill of such words; they suddenly awaken "indisposed," and out come all those thorns. When that happens, usually after the honeymoon when the bee has lost its sting, you begin to hear talk of incompatibility, of personality differences—personality being what we call "character." But like the rose on the table or the windowsill, women continue to play a major role here; their influence, like their perfume, fills the air. In fact, their hold on things is so great that when a man needs advice, he turns to his wife, for she's the one who controls the purse strings. Is he being solicitous? Well, he may solicit the advice of his wife, but she advises him in such a way that he thinks he came to the decision all by himself; after all, he's the only one who's allowed to bang the table with his fist. If women enjoy such a powerful position in this society, it's because they wear pants—what they now call culottes. But to an observer, it makes no difference what you call them or whether they're made of the finest nylon or not—pants are pants.

When the man takes all the covers at night, the woman fights back by giving him casseroles. And so, the Visigoth side emerges once more. Some say it's the Alaman side surfacing to reclaim its rightful place in the scheme of things. Anyhow, to satisfy this side of their nature too, Parisians don't mind their children playing war even if they themselves don't particularly like it. They've been this way for ages.

Since their grandparents played war, the children must follow in the same footsteps; they too must learn to kill soldiers with bullets. At the same time they vote against war, they buy revolvers for their kids. Don't bother trying to get them to explain this behavior; their answers would shatter your own beliefs and convictions. They know how to turn a phrase to get people on their side. In fact, they know how to use their language so well they've even opened schools specializing in rhetoric and debate.

From time to time they come to blows with their neighbors over the right-of-way on a river or the matter of who controls the western part of a town that straddles two borders. There are several towns and waterways like this; the former are in areas of perennial conflict, the latter, following quietly along their courses, laugh at the whole question of who owns what. Each side defends itself by saying its individual rights and freedom are at stake. Each side not only uses the same words and calls the other liar but also says prayers and burns candles so that God and the saints might award it a victory. To awaken the saints and get them going, to mobilize them for the greater good of the country, the people might even blow a bugle in the middle of a mass. The effect of such action on the nerves would be so great that the saints, caught off guard, would certainly see to it that the side which uses this tactic first would win. I think you'll agree that this probably would never happen, but with these people you never know. There might be some truth to it, for where there's smoke, there's sure to be fire. But let's face it, since the terms "individual rights" and "freedom" mean, for some, wife, children, and home, and for others, an entire way of life—the whole kit and caboodle of habits and customs—each side is bound to set off bravely to fight "one last time."

Those who dare to give the terms "individual rights" and "freedom" other meanings are accused of being traitors and are thrown in prison. Then, of course, events change course; the prisoners are freed, and once they take over, they put those who had accused them in prison. It's hard to keep track of what happens here and even harder to figure out a people who attach more importance to the most banal suggestion of their leader than to an accident that might do away with twenty people in one fell swoop. Curious folks, these people. They say they're sick and tired of war, and yet they're always preparing for it, down to the last detail. And you never can distinguish the leader of an insurrection from the leader of a rebellion. When an Alaman or a Parisian revolts against the whole way of life they inherited from the past, it's called an insurrection, but when that past revolts against the Parisians, it's called a rebellion. And if the Goths take control of a bit of woods or a hilltop in order to reclaim certain rights from the Parisians who threaten to stifle them, they're called rebels; when this happens, the Visigoths, long oppressed because they were first to arrive here, take note and find themselves up against the combined weight of the Goths, Alamans, and Franks; and if they manage to unseat the Parisians, they become pirates. A real puzzle, all this! Nothing more than a slight difference in meaning, they say, nothing more than traffic signals that change from red to green! When you reach the point where you simply can't understand, you end up shouting, "Oh, those Parisians! They lie through their teeth!" Yes, my friend, they hide their true feelings. This way they can appear warm without really being so; they can be like pastel colors and muted perfumes—nothing can blind or offend you. It all amounts to their being "unto themselves."

They're so "unto themselves," in fact, that they all walk at the same pace. Even the women. When two Parisians are seen leaving a store, as soon as they cross the threshold, their feet—hesitating only momentarily because of the bright light—move into synchronized step. It's a habit they learned from being in the service. That may be true for the men, but what about the women? They also try to be in tune with each other. You'll notice that in a cafe, for example, two or three of them will be yawning at the same time, or smoking. They'll pass the lighter from one to the other, stare in unison at a pretty woman, or read the newspaper, and they all have a cup of coffee or a glass of something in front of them. Like good friends, honest and forthright, Parisians are always asking for a vote of confidence: "Do you want to be like me?" "Do you want to join me?" If you agree to this, you'll end up following along right to the end. You'll share everything. And don't think for a minute they'll be wary of you. They were honest in asking you to join them, to link arms, and if you don't share, they'll consider you inferior. They don't like barriers between themselves and others. And yet, these people who love to share always keep the doors to their homes shut tight. You might be neighbors, but they'll ignore you for years at a time. They don't want to meddle in the affairs of others and don't want you meddling in theirs. They barely notice you, and if they do, it's just that they don't want to be stared at. But the women less so. As soon as they think someone's looking at them, they adjust their dresses, close their purses, pass their hands over their hair, and lower their eyelids. Then they divert their attention and glance at you out of the corner of their eye, as if to say, "How impolite!" Yet they have such beautiful eyes that you could linger there and be impolite forever and ever.

When you arrive in Paris, in this Paris that lives underground, in the metro, be sure to buy a map of the city. It won't help you at all in the beginning, but you need to have one. All tourists do this. Then be sure to get yourself a map of the metro. Another wasted expense, but get one anyway. Armed with this map, proceed to lose yourself in the maze of corridors and arrows, of signs and crowds and wrong ways, ascents and descents; don't get on the train you should but the one you shouldn't; then go into another station, exit, enter again, and march up to a ticket-puncher and explain that you're lost; take off and lose yourself once more. Finally, walk out and head down the street right in front of you. Only by doing all this will you be able to call yourself Parisian, for you will have learned what the signs and corridors and hand signals mean. You'll have learned to run so that you won't miss the train you want or have the door slam shut smack in your face. You'll even learn the shortcuts in time. And soon you'll move automatically toward an exit or a connecting train, and you'll have learned not to try to open and close doors—they are also automatic. All these little details will show just how much Paris has become part of you, has assimilated you. The Parisians aren't very talkative or effervescent; you might say they're a rather sedate sort of people who tolerate everything but live unto themselves in their city of light. In fact, they're lights themselves, lights among the other lights of Paris. They let you walk beside them, they let you live in their light, but don't think for a minute that you can love Paris more than they do. Paris is part of them; it's in their blood. If Paris exists it's because the Parisians exist, and they watch over their city in the same way Saint Geneviève does. These people are completely caught up in the idea of freedom, and they aim to enjoy its advantages. Their sense of fairness is such that they've even imprinted it on their machines, which are "made in the same mold" so to speak—that is, they have the same habits, the same way of thinking. Example: their public telephones return your coin if you haven't been able to get through. They've ordered life in such a way that everyone can enjoy it. Despite this, however, there are still those unfortunate ones who decide to end their lives by jumping into the Seine. And yet all of Paris seems to sing life's pleasures: the trees and flowers, the smiles on the faces of the women, the whir of cars, a wedding procession, all the fountains and pigeons, and even the constant prattle of tourists armed with binoculars and cameras. Even things that shouldn't move manage to fool the foreigner now and then.

When you see all the people on the streets you're convinced there's no one left at home. It's like an anthill. But a window will open, and sure enough a head appears. The more I wander around the city, the more confused I get. I'm not used to it yet. It's an impregnable city that sweeps you up, flattens you, and then returns you to the world with a label on your collar—a label that's assigned to you and establishes who you are, a mark of civility that will allow you to go anywhere and maintain your status, your status as a Parisian. You're "Made in Paris." Everyone here is on stage and plays a role, from the scientist in his laboratory busy studying diseases to the early morning star shining its light upon those who frequent the nightspots. Since the dead are considered capable of further action, they too are recruited for the show: to hold the hands of the living. If Paris is impregnable, it's surely because these forces are in conjunction. Oarsmen in the sailing ships of yesteryear, the Parisians have become the driving force of the great sailing ship that Paris is today! And to make sure nothing threatens the absolute accord that exists among five million people, each with different dreams, they have erected around themselves a barrier of hands that assist each other whenever and wherever they need to. Thus, the commissioner of police lends a hand to the judge, a policeman to a process server or a prison warden; and all this occurs without violating whatsoever the peoples' sovereign rights. You lend a hand, nothing more. And lending isn't always giving, or holding. Hands that've become accustomed to lending find it in their best interest to stay together, to join and create a barrier so strong that people wind up talking about a partisan government. But partisan on which side? Since when is a government not partisan? Since when doesn't it serve a particular group? Since when doesn't it serve the people who live under its rule and for whom it exists in the first place? If it changes hands, it simply goes from being partisan on one side to being partisan on the other. That's why their government is always searching for stability. Just when it's at the point of falling, they ask for what they call a formal "vote of confidence." This is a little bit like what we do when we openly express our grief for a dying relative. On a day set aside expressly for this purpose—I don't know how they do this— the government leaders, in full dress, meet to discuss matters. Everyone says what they think: what they think is good, what they think is bad. After everyone has had a chance to speak his mind, the moment arrives when all must decide—by vote—the fate of the government. On one side are all those who want the government to fall; on the other, those who want it to continue. Most often the latter win. If the former win, the government falls and their party takes over. And what do we find? The same men have simply changed seats; they've simply changed duties.

But there are those who are to the government what our charging bulls are back home. They never leave it alone; they keep piercing it until it dies. These people are called "politicians." They're so adept at what they do you never know which foot to dance on. They're so smooth, so supple, they slip through everything and anything without ever getting caught. They can topple a government in two minutes and establish another one in "five secs." I'm not quite sure what this expression means, but it has a good ring to it, and if I use it I sound like a Parisian. In "five secs." You're always learning something here, even as you watch the policemen, who, by the by, have the remarkable title of peace officer. You see their smile more often than you do the club they carry, but still, peace on earth must be armed. Despite the fact that they labor under enormous pressure, whenever you speak to one they're not at all patronizing but salute you as one man to another. Whether you're in the street, in the metro, or on a bus, they're always there, standing straight and tall. And they send you on your way with a smile. It's so easy to lose sight of the road to peace that the Parisians have posted an officer at every intersection to point it out to you. Those Parisians think of everything to help you. But the people here who seem to thrive on conflict—do they even notice the peace officers? They're forever stirring up old fires and starting new ones. By doing this they're following those their own consciences see as having real authority, and here everyone has their own special preferences. This is so embedded in their nature that whenever someone wants to exchange anonymity for the limelight, the first questions they're asked are "Who is your favorite author? Whom do you admire most?" Everyone then calls to the fore one or the other of those now dead. There might be several people they could summon, but one will stand out and serve as the model. If you're faced with making a decision, you ask yourself, What would the master have done? And even if the master might have shifted his customary way of thinking in this particular situation, your answer would reflect his usual behavior. You'd remain true to what he stood for; you'd do so on principle. But most of the time, people who act on such principles don't have principles of their own. Honor the master! This is not to say, however, that the Parisians can't make decisions on their own. Careful, don't force me to say what I don't want to say. I simply want to emphasize the close ties that exist between the Parisians now and those of yesterday and before. They join hands with those from the past. All this makes Paris truly difficult to know. And yet you must try. You must let yourself become a part of her: her five million inhabitants, her stones and monuments and famous sewers, the flowers on the windowsills, the hoops the children play with, the mannerisms of the café waiters, the temper tantrums of the maids, the French fries, the fast pace and the slow-moving Seine; and even more, you must become a part of the several million dead whom the city watches over. All this makes the city at once noisy yet quiet, light yet heavy, rich yet poor. There'll be a bustling avenue on one side of you, a sleepy one adjacent to it; over here, a bright and shiny fairyland, over there only a few lights. There'll be singing and games and incessant noise farther on, but in the quarter nearby everything will be quiet and respectable, draped in the solemnity of the past, and the wind that passes through such quarters wears slippers so as to show proper reverence. You'll learn from experience that the dead are the people most alive here; you not only meet them at every intersection, you hear them invoked in the high courts and academies, indeed cited throughout the day. The Parisians are obsessed with collecting things—rocks, insects, plants, pottery; and they put it all in huge halls they call museums, which they adore visiting. Despite their carefree attitude, they do worry about the future and love to keep track of what they've accomplished. Yet when they look at the Arch of Triumph, the Elysée palace, the Tuileries, Versailles, or Vincennes, they're always complaining about their fall from Grace. They'd love to have the power and influence of those who've entered the race only recently, forgetting the fact that they've been around a long time, that experience alone doesn't make a man—or even a nation—fly. They say their walls are gray! But what do they expect after so many hands have touched them to test their solidity?

They're a levelheaded and thrifty people too; they take in everything, even the smoke from the factories. A people who hate waste. Here, even the garbage that's collected every morning has a role to play, a job to do, a space to fill. And everything happens so fast that you no longer have the time to wait for someone underneath the wonderful shade of an elm tree, even if that wait were in vain.

In one of their museums, the Grévin, I saw the straw hat their greatest emperor, Napoleon, wore on the island of Saint Helena; I also saw the desk where he worked. Here was a man who, during his days of glory, wrote on a marble desk in a palace; he would never have consented to own a simple wooden desk, no matter the price. The Parisians have never pardoned this effrontery, and to emphasize the fact that the emperor has lost nothing of his glory, that delusions of grandeur aren't easily dismissed, all around his statue in the Place Vendôme are the famous fashion designers, who continue to dress the Parisians in elegant clothes, the perfumers who make them smell good, and the jewelers who adorn them in precious jewels. All for the sake of glory . . . I saw the bathtub where Marat was assassinated. Here was a man who felt the enormous pressures of a regime he detested, a man on the side of the people, who cried with them and flailed their persecutors with his writings. His ruthless behavior during the king's trial made him bitterly hated. Thus, he was assassinated. I saw Mirabeau. His huge head still seems to be bubbling with ideas, and you think you can hear him bursting forth once more with his famous address.

He had the courage of a lion, but given his lack of money, he needed the help of the king and queen. He was revered by the people, and they were ready to die for him; and when he died, he was carried in triumph to the Pantheon. And yet, when the people found out about his relationship with the court, they removed him and put Marat in his place. They're still there, however, the wax figures of Marat and Mirabeau. They may be silent now, but they still offer a profound lesson to those in this city who can read and listen, who can truly comprehend what both represented. The Parisians may give the appearance of being frivolous, and their city may have districts famous the world over for their fads and fashion, but they're deeply in love with virtue and know how to honor their true advocates. Foreigners, however, are deceived because they must settle for the surface of things. But Parisians know full well that truth is never easily visible, never easily discerned, that it hides itself under a veil. And when they talk of truth and virtue, they use a language that's also veiled. This is the language the foreigner always hears, and you can only respond on that level. The Parisians, on the other hand, were initiated into this secret language from the start; it's in their nature. Their history is a part of them, and they live it everyday. Whatever they do, whether they're going or coming, running, working, laughing, dancing, or sitting, they straighten up fast as soon as anyone threatens to show disrespect for that history, orally or in writing. They grab their slingshots and muskets, set pens to paper, summon all the resources they can, and force the disrespect out of you. And then, as if nothing had happened, they continue on where they'd left off, following the direction their dreams take them, acting nice on the telephone once more. How can you recognize a Parisian? Easy. When the telephone rings, they grab pencil and paper, unhook the receiver, and immediately start doodling as they listen. If it's an elderly Parisian, he'll draw a castle in a beautiful countryside, with perhaps a river running by and a bird in the sky, and two or three nicely dressed people. Those who draw lines and squares or dots and dashes are the young Parisians who haven't yet assimilated their history. To the tourist who visits Paris and who, by chance, is thrown off scent and ends up in the Grévin Museum, where you're tempted to "see more with your fingers than with your eyes," Paris, her proud history before her, seems to say, "Courage, my friend. This is progress. I was once at the stage you are now. I knew Attila the Hun. I've been destroyed several times, but each time the Parisians have rolled up their sleeves, taken pickaxes and trowels in hand, and, with sweat on their brows, seen the buildings appear once again, stone by stone. You may think I'm old and cold-blooded. Wrong. My blood is as warm as that of the people who live in the tropics."

The air is so charged with electricity that tensions surface frequently. This is true even when the sun doesn't shine. You often see bands of people marching against those who call themselves communist, people who don't believe in either God or the devil. Isn't it shocking to find communists in a place where everything—every stone—reflects the light of the Cross? The faithful, that new breed of crusader, armed supposedly with tolerance, often set off to storm the strongholds of communist activity. Each side fights for its own particular beliefs. I can't help but wonder about those communists, who can look at the sky and earth and believe that all came from nothing. But I suppose it's hard to fault them since from the time they were born their parents have told them that children come from storks. If this is true, why then do we need God? Cartesian logic. But the faithful try to prove His exis-tence by beating on the doors of communist strongholds, by burning their journals and splitting their heads open. These tactics, however, have only produced dry results. And yet, the same things keep happening; they continue to believe that force will make the communists under-stand the errors of their ways. Surely the communists will come to understand that they must seek heaven not earth, that water is more important than bread. Surely they will learn this and become strong supporters of such beliefs. Everyone here waits for this miracle to happen. What bothers me most, perhaps, is that we keep saying God made every person an individual, and yet we want to force everyone to march in the same direction. We've done this for centuries. Never once has God made any effort to force us to think alike. Isn't this His way of disapproving of what we're doing? Don't think this is simply a Parisian matter; we have this problem too.

Here's Talleyrand. This priest did as much as a member of Parliament would to make the nation favorably disposed to the interests of the clergy. He's the one who introduced Bonaparte to the Directory. He'd go from one side to another without even moving; he pushed Bonaparte into the arms of Marie Louise and then left them on their own while he sought the favors of Louis XVIII. After Waterloo he lived under all sorts of different regimes and managed to survive, the perfect political animal: shrewd, slippery. The Parisians still consider him an enigma. Beside him, his friend Fouché. Both lived through intensely troubled times; both were intimately involved in events where even the slightest slip of the tongue could mean the guillotine—and yet both of them died in bed. These two men are considered true leaders by many Parisians. And the Parisians are an intelligent people, are they not? Well, at least they've learned not to spit on the ground or blow their noses in their hands. Instead, they use tiny squares of cloth that factories here seem to provide in abundance. You see them thrust their hands in their pockets, and what do you think comes out? A handkerchief, my friend, a handkerchief to spit in, to blow their noses in; and after they're through, they carefully fold it and put it back in their pockets. People make a fortune not only seeing to it that they're well dressed but provided with material for their noses and mouths as well.

And these people had as their leaders Talleyrand and Fouché. It's almost impossible to understand. If I understand anything, it's that they build their fortunes on the back of time. They do this by running. They even run when they're seated in a cafe drinking beer in little sips like birds. But don't worry, time won't find them there. They'll be off before you know it, off to decide how to save what they earn by not living a full life.

SINCE TODAY is Sunday, I figured the people would follow the dictates of their church and take the day off, as we do back home when our fetishists tell us that Mondays and Fridays are days of rest. Well, the Parisians may get up a bit later than usual, but once up, they immediately start working. Here, then, Sundays are no different from other days—they're just as hectic.

With wings fluttering nonstop, pigeons take their baths in whatever waterholes present themselves. There are always a few kind souls around to give them seed out of their hands. With pigeons perched on their shoulders and hovering all about them, you have a perfect picture of mutual understanding. Pigeons seem to belong to Paris; they're involved in everything that goes on—so much so, that their absence would cause many a Parisian to suffer. I must confess it's a beautiful sight, those birds flying down from the trees, sipping water from the fountains, attacking the seed, and literally glueing themselves to their benefactors as if to thank them for remembering their needs. It's impossible to calculate just how grateful they are; the sum would be too great. And to think children don't even throw rocks at them! Cats, dogs, whatever—it's astonishing how much these people love animals. But the Parisians also consider the cat a bad omen, a symbol of deceit and treachery—especially the black cat. No matter how much purring it does, this animal will never be completely trusted by these people. They'll play with it, but they'll never forget they're playing with a cat, the most dangerous of animals. And if you hear them talking about "still water," you can bet they're referring to a cat. To help stress the point, we can give them one of our expressions: "He's meaner than a black cat." Sometimes they'll even compare the cat to a snake, a viper, and as deadly too. As you can see, it makes no difference where you live, no one likes surprise attacks—or treachery of any sort for that matter. The Parisians may enjoy being a bit sly now and then, but honesty and candor are still highly prized, are still considered virtues. In fact, snakes are so hated that even Christ's mother would love to crush one with her foot. And the day will come when even the black cat will get its comeuppance. It won't always be able to pull in its claws whenever it wants to. Here's a little story to show you just how much

41

Parisians love their cats. I walked into a friend's house. Their dog growled at me. My friend kept yelling, "Come on in, he won't bite!" I wasn't so sure, given the size of those teeth. But I went on in, sat down, and began to fondle the cat that had jumped into my lap. My friend looked at me and said, "That's the one with the mean streak, you know." I knew I'd walked right into the trap. I too had fallen for the sweet, smiling face, those soft purring sounds, the warm round shape ...

It's obvious Parisians find an enormous difference between the perfidious cat and that symbol of honest and true friendship—the dog. In fact, dogs are so adored they have their own beauty parlors. You see so many men and women walking dogs you're not always sure who's leading whom. Sometimes it's the dog who makes them run, who pulls them this way or that; sometimes it's the people who take control. Here people talk to dogs in the same way they talk to children—something they don't do with cats—and those who own dogs won't even eat until they're sure their pets have eaten. Such excessive attention would bother even the most devoted husband or wife. Here people seem more interested in you if you show an interest in their pets, much as we do when we coddle up to children whose mothers we want to like us. I even saw a venerable old gentleman let himself be licked by a puppy— that's what they call a baby dog. This puppy licked him on the cheeks and nose, all over his eyes and forehead. In return, the man gave it cookies and candy. We'd rarely see this back home. Imagine letting yourself be licked all over by an animal, even one as faithful as a dog! Imagine stuffing it with sweets! Why that would cause a scandal! But not here. Here dogs and cats—in fact, all pets—curl up on chairs, beds, even the most elegant armchairs, and no one seems to mind. No one says a word.

Why such love for animals? To pay homage to their ancestors. Yes, it's true. In this enlightened country, this temple of scientific wisdom, Parisians have no trouble seeing man as superior to the boar and billy goat, but not to the monkey they descended from and certainly not to the dog—that symbol of loyalty expressly put in animal form so that man would have an example to learn from. Yes, they believe the monkey is their ancestor; in fact, they're so convinced of their simian ancestry, so caught up at the same time with the progress they've made that you'll often hear them say, "Oh, come on now! Quit acting like a monkey!" What they really mean is, don't monkey around with their ancestor. Show some respect for it. After all, his age demands it. I hesitate to say this, but when I happen to see certain white chests with all those black hairs, something inside me whispers, They may be right. The monkey calls up such fear in them that whenever they tell a child to stop acting like one, the child turns into a human being. He doesn't scratch himself anymore, he doesn't turn somersaults or make funny faces. They consider their ancestor so special they've even put chains around it. A strange way, indeed, to honor one's origins! In truth, the monkey is simply a monkey; it doesn't demand the same reverence a mother or father does. . . . But sometimes I catch myself wondering if the Parisians haven't put chains around our simian ancestor as well—the ancestor of those who are black, yellow, and red. After all, up to now, no one has ever seen a white monkey. Scientists continue trying to unravel the mysterious link between monkeys and people despite the fact that such study goes against the formal teachings of their church, which says that man was created by God in God's image. Those who take issue with such teachings, on the other hand, argue that monkeys evolved from angels. Equipped with wings and dressed in white robes, angels are considered the intermediaries between God and man. Long white robes must definitely play a special role in this country since many people wear them—angels, saints, priests, lawyers, judges, women. . . . It's the women, naturally, who wear them best of all. And then you're told about all the different names and tribes, the different ranks and duties of the angels. All this is designed to confirm the hypothesis that God indeed lives among us. Like us, the angels are also separated into two camps: there are the good angels and the bad angels. The good angels are white; the bad angels are black. The black ones are called devils. I keep wondering if the Parisian is an angel, if I am a devil. It's frightening to consider the influence such rigid classifications continue to have on people's attitudes. And yet they do . . . How well I know.

Some people when they see me think they've encountered the devil himself. Funny, I had no idea I was that black! And yet I'm used to this now. It just goes to show that some people aren't very good at discriminating one color from another. But should we even broach the subject of color? Here God is white; that's all there is to it. But what color do we make Him? . . . Yes, it's true, I scare people—especially women and children. They see me coming and immediately try to escape; there's no getting beyond the initial impression. The only thing that matters is what they see. I catch them by surprise. That's the problem. They must wonder what in the world possessed God to get the colors wrong and smear me with tar? What allows me to draw near again and convinces them that God must have been bewitched is my white teeth. Of course,

racism

it's my dark skin that makes them look whiter than they really are. Maybe that's what fascinates them, what draws them toward me. My white teeth, thick lips, and coal-black skin! I'm a problem for them, a puzzle, and they can't make heads or tails of it—something they haven't been able to do since they lost touch with their Roman past.

Parisians hate the idea of a devil rebelling against God, but, at the same time, they hate the idea of someone playing the part of an angel—especially doing so on earth. They have a saying: "He who wants to be an angel is a fool." I must admit I don't understand how "fool" and "angel" go together. Is what they say an invitation to live fully, to make the most of every moment and grab all we can—even steal a kiss that lips may, or may not, offer? I wonder. We've got to remember that everything the Parisians say must be picked apart and analyzed carefully; otherwise, you pass right by what they really mean. And yet, even if you don't manage to understand completely, even if what they say has no meaning to you whatsoever, you still end up weighing their words. Christ once said, "Happy are the poor in spirit." But not in Paris! Oh no, not here! The Parisians go to any lengths to be rich in spirit. In fact, they've got spirit to spare! To save face, they always let you know where they stand—they're always ready with an opinion. And they never lose their temper, even if someone is curt with them. With them, life's a constant jousting match, and "spirit" is the name of the game. That's the nature of conversation in this city. Those who aren't rich in spirit, those who aren't quick with an answer—why there's no way they sustain the pitch. No, not here, not in Paris. Lorded over as it is by Saint Geneviève, and forever nurturing, honing its "spirit," Paris has never heard God's words. But let's return to the subject of angels.

*

* *

To save His chosen people, it is said that God sent a band of angels to exterminate the Egyptians. The wings of those divine creatures were covered with the blood of the innocent children they slaughtered. But weren't the Egyptians also created by God? Weren't they, too, created in His image? These are the questions that remain unanswered; these are the questions you keep asking yourself in this city of light and glitter. I'm convinced that when the people here pray, they do so to clear their consciences. I'm not sure you can believe everything they say or bet money on it either, for that matter. And yet, we can't forget that Beelzebub, prince of devils, keeps watch over those sinners who are doomed to burn forever and ever on a lake of fire, which, since the beginning of time, has never been extinguished. I'm sure that's why Parisians are so pious and race off to mass every Sunday—they want to make sure their skin stays white. The doors to their churches are always closed, like the gates to paradise, but they're never locked. Apparently these good people never for a moment forget the perpetual fire that could await them. If Saint Peter holds the keys to paradise, it's so that people down below won't want to risk punishment by fire. Hell may be a domain apart, but an isolated ash or two may leap up and fall on the head of an unbeliever. Women in long black robes and large white headdresses, umbrellas over their arms, walk among the faithful. Each one carries a book or a rosary. All of a sudden they'll stop and lift their eyes toward the frescoes on the ceiling, as if looking for the source of what they call "grace," that gift of salvation God promises those who stay on the right path. You discover that the apple—associated as it is with original sin—is one of the prime resources of the country. The fruit of the forbidden tree is not only cultivated by the faithful, it's found on every hassock, on every tongue. It's said that when God created the world, He created a garden in the middle of that world, and in the middle of that garden an apple tree. Confined there were our ancestors Adam and Eve—the monkey doesn't figure here—and they were absolutely forbidden to eat the fruit of that tree. The fruit was so inviting that merely looking at it made your mouth water. But no! They were forbidden to touch it! It took a serpent with a forked tongue to trick our illustrious ancestors. And ever since, these people who love to play tricks on each other, who call each other "my little chick," "my little chickadee," say of those who speak ill of another, "They have the tongue of a serpent." Adam and Eve found the apple so good, however, that they kept eating it, singing all the while.

I must admit that this magnificent fruit is being sold today by young girls who are no less magnificent. Their smile alone is worth more than the flattery of a thousand snakes—why even one tiny wink is enough to make you eat a ton of apples! And so the world has gone ever since Adam ate that apple. It's a burden we all share—happily so!

A man with a walking cane—he must be important given the hat he wears, the braid on his shoulders, and the bandolier across his chest—walks back and forth, his eyes glued to the priest who, from his place on high, begs God to bless the faithful who've come to pray, to shine

His light on them and their misery. Those gathered below lay everything at God's feet: their dreams and disappointments, whatever is on their mind—debts, taxes, even an argument they may have had. Acting as God's official interpreter, the priest or parish priest or abbot opens his arms and gathers them up, whispers phrases his assistants then repeat in unison, kneels, and stands up again. Nothing escapes the verger who walks back and forth; nothing escapes the women in black who, collection plates in hand, circulate among the faithful. Everyone gives what they can. No one's obliged to give anything, but they feel it a moral responsibility to pay to worship. It's only fair that God have a beautiful house here on earth, one filled with the smell of incense and decorated with splendid gilt work.

Statues of saints line the walls, but among them not one black. I repeat: not one black. We haven't yet earned the right to a place in paradise. Our skin color must have really frightened Saint Peter because he steered us instead toward Beelzebub. He must have taken us for a marauding army of devils ready to pick a quarrel about nothing. You almost believe it's because of us that he always carries his keys. He's afraid we'll spread trouble among the peaceful inhabitants of paradise—such hard-won peace, after all, must be kept at all costs. But trouble is precisely what we've had by remaining in our own backyards. Let's hope that when we're better known we too will acquire a saint. But then, the devil will have to assume another color, and that won't be an easy thing to do.

A saint is someone who's earned a special place in heaven for having scrupulously obeyed not only God's ten commandments but the seven the Church has as well. Following in the footsteps of Paris itself, loaded down as it is with saints, other cities have fought to have their own special people occupy a similar position. The women who take up the collection are called "sisters." Among them are "mothers" and "mothers superior." They've dedicated themselves to educating the young, and they're unflagging in that mission. Most of the faithful are women, and most of them wear wedding rings. They receive this piece of jewelry the day they're married to show they've been "surrounded," to remind them that their passion must be given to one man only—their husband. They've been "walled off," so to speak, and no others will be allowed to breach the circle of defense. After the ceremony at the mayor's office, where the marriage is officially sanctioned and where the bride and groom promise to love each other always—this is an important part of the contract—they head for the church. There a priest will bless the union and make it valid in the eyes of God. Bells ring out as if to say: "There's still time to change your mind. Look around, seek further advice, examine your heart and mind carefully. Don't go into this lightly." Nothing here is done by accident; everything has a meaning, and you don't move without knowing what that meaning is. The priest wears white to attest to the innocence of those being married. He lights the candles in order for the union to truly shine—he wants everything to be perfect. If the flames burn steadily, calmly, the marriage will reflect the same ongoing brilliance. Great precaution is needed in case things go otherwise, for, as the Mass dictates, if a candle is extinguished, so is the possibility of any recourse. In God's eyes there is no such thing as divorce. He considers such marital problems as incompatibility, sterility, the wicked deeds of one spouse or the other insufficient reasons to argue they're not suited to each other. He might have stressed the need to "be fruitful and multiply," to fill the entire earth with the noise of our laughter, our songs and dances, for they too are as much a part of our life as are our lamentations. But if at home everyone has the right to marry, here the priest must remain celibate. Moreover, no one can have two husbands or two wives. They have very strict moral codes here: don't covet a woman no matter how beautiful she is; don't keep looking at her since looking breeds desire; don't get too near since that would be like putting fire to gunpowder; don't touch her or smell her perfume or hold her hand—all these things will give you unclean thoughts, that is, thoughts not deemed quite Catholic. But even if you manage to keep true to the ten commandments, for sure you'll slip on one of the seven the Church has. That seems to be the role of the priest here: to watch over us, married or not. He's everyone's confidant; people tell him things they'd ordinarily only tell God. Feuillantines, Capuchins, Trappists, Jesuits, Templars, Cistercians, Dominicans, Sulpicians—all these various sects, and others besides, unite in condemning us because our beliefs are different from theirs. Did God institute only one system of worship? Did He command us all to think alike? It seems these people prefer bringing God down to their own level rather than really trying to understand Him and His ways.

The Parisian may be courteous, but he's not always so when it comes to women. That's because all these sects wage merciless battle on this front. One of them—one of the better known—has even written, "Mischief breeds underneath the prettiest, most angelic of faces." I don't want to give them further reason for believing this, but isn't there a little genie inside each one who delights in hurting those tender souls who love them the most, who thwart any attempt at conversation? They're swift in refusing you, so swift, in fact, that you wonder if, underneath their haughty exteriors, they're even capable of love, capable of letting themselves go—if they're even able to cry if someone spurns them.

Yes, today is Sunday, my first Sunday in Paris. People pass by with their eyes glued to a newspaper—everyone here buys a newspaper. Things happen fast, and the Parisians are determined to keep up. No one has yet blown cigarette smoke in my face or shaken the dust from their rugs on my head. Elderly couples are seated in gardens, enjoying the fresh air. Young girls stroll along, their mothers close by. It's a nice sight—these young girls hand in hand.

LINING THE STREETS are mailboxes, benches, and trees providing a bit of shade. Every single cafe is jam-packed with people—couples, young women, and one or two men sitting by themselves. Several women keep staring into the distance—they're obviously waiting for someone. They've opened and closed their purses at least twenty times, folded, unfolded, and refolded their newspapers, and checked their watches every few seconds. One has put on some lipstick; another has redone her makeup two or three times. Still another one has made a telephone call and returned to her chair. Nothing has happened; only time marches on. How do the people kill time here? Here they do, believe me, and all the time they're doing it, they lament they're losing money! They kill time in all conceivable ways—they read, daydream, drink, dance. Everyone enjoys killing time—the rich, the poor, and those in between. And yet, they'd all like to strangle it—some, because it forces them to waste fifteen minutes, others because it passes too fast, still others because it either moves too slow or pays no attention to them, but most simply because it's fun to kill time. But time just laughs at them, for just when they think they've killed it, the moment has long passed. Yes, time just laughs; it's always beyond peoples' reach.

The women keep waiting, getting more and more restless. When a woman waits in this country, she does so with her whole heart, with every nerve and muscle. What exhilaration people feel in this country when they know that a young woman is waiting for them. Her eyes are riveted to the street. She checks out every car that stops; she searches the crowds for you. They act as if they're sitting on hot coals. I adore this sort of exhilaration: it gives you confidence; it makes you feel you're in control of things.

In the sweetest voice possible I began talking to a young woman sitting next to me. I had many things churning in my head, dancing on the tip of my tongue, and they all came tumbling out: the beauty of our country with its springs, the music of the bamboo trees and the birds, the whisperings of the sugar cane, the play of light on the leaves—what can I say, my friend? I talked of everything and nothing. The sort of nothing women love. She couldn't read my thoughts because my skin is black. What can one do to overcome the difference? They'd like to

49

relegate me to a dark corner, somewhere away from the heart of things, but I don't let them. And to make sure I don't let them, I show them my hand: "See, I don't have a wedding ring." "Yes, we see," their looks seem to say, "but do you have that custom in your country?" I nod my head. They, in turn, nod back, smiling, as if my nod had been some sort of salutation. They're good-natured souls, nonetheless. I look at them and proceed passionately: "See how I burn? My eyes are red, my body scorched!" I might as well be speaking Greek! But they don't hear. Unlike us, they're not tuned into words unspoken. With heads held high and eyes pointed upward, they switch their purses from one shoulder to the other and prepare to leave. Cautious souls! On fire as I am, I risk burning them. They pass. I smile the sort of smile we do back home when we want . . . well, you know . . . But they continue on. My smile reaches from ear to ear. Pooh! They don't even acknowledge it. I'm beginning to wonder whether those Boeotians[1] there are really from Paris. They lack a certain dash, a certain oomph.

I've been told that conversation becomes possible if you begin by talking about the weather or if you ask for a light or offer a cigarette or a cup of coffee. Sometimes God really knows how to do things! Just then, an absolutely splendid young woman sat down at the table next to mine. She breathed deeply, opened her purse to get a mirror, examined her hair and face, and then ordered a "demi." That's what they say here when they want a glass of beer. She tossed her head as if to get rid of a thought that kept pestering her. No wedding ring. She looked around. Her eyes hit mine. What beautiful shoulders! What curves! She had a gorgeous head of hair, marvelous breasts! Perfect, she was, from any angle, any perspective.

"It threatened to rain yesterday."

No response.

"But today is beautiful."

Again no response.

"Let's hope it continues this way."

Still no response. Has she suddenly become dumb?

"Don't you agree?"

No answer.

I'm told that you're supposed to keep insisting, to keep pulling the rope until she gives in. But when actually faced with an instance like

---

1. As used here, the word "Boeotian" refers to people without cultural refinement, a bit dull or stupid.

this, is it really better to insist? You risk being taken for a farmhand. Maybe she doesn't like talking about the weather; after all, each of us has something bad to say about it. Let me try breaking the ice with the match trick.

"Cigarette?"

"Thank you."

Ah yes, my friend, it's working. It's working. I merely need to fan the fire to keep things burning. But what am I saying? She withdraws; her face darkens. With elbows on the table, she lights the cigarette and stares off into the distance. She must be part of the Maginot Line. A feminine fortress that needs to be stormed. A typical female—that is, a woman who makes you bleed simply to give you something to do to take your mind off her. So there you sit, nursing the wound she gave you.

Finally, he's arrived. Glowing smiles brighten their faces; they blush. Their blood is the type that moves upward easily. You read everything in their faces: hate, love, anger. As if to discover who's eaten and drunk what, these two lovers kiss each other on the mouth. What joy they must feel! Each is a part of the other. It's a custom they can't undo, for its roots are firmly anchored in tradition.

Everyone here smokes. And they use the tobacco they themselves grow. What clever souls! There are also more women who smoke than there are back home. But I've never seen them chew it; if they do, they do it in such a way that you can't tell. And always the mass of cars and pedestrians. It's like an anthill where everyone complains about being a worker. But you've got to admire these people and their determination not to bother each other, to let everyone go their own way. And so, I'm sitting alone. If someone takes a seat next to me, they never fail to ask, "Sir, is this chair occupied?" They're a polite people who'll just as politely leave you alone in your corner as long as you want to stay there. They might help you now and then, but as long as it doesn't take them out of their way. And that's the problem: not to take them out of their way! With us this isn't always so, but with some, it is. Parisians take their time to know you since deep down inside there's still a bit of distrust.

The Parisians know the price of freedom better than anyone else, and you see this love for freedom in everything they do. When they smoke, they breathe in full force, and when they shake the ashes off their cigarettes, they do so with authority—as if to say, "So there!"

Centuries of struggle have given them the right to be themselves, to be out from under; thus, they have the right to consume as much salt as they want, to bake their bread wherever they want. These are little things, to be sure, but they help make life worthwhile. And it's the little things that make you feel like a human being. Is it really true that the freest people in the world are those who are able to control the passions that always threaten to enslave them? If Parisians always cross their legs, it's simply because they're tired of walking, and they're not going to be forced to do so if they don't want to. Centuries of history have made them this way. Don't talk to them about civil or military glory—the time to do so has long passed. They know its price; they know its burden. If they read their newspapers so carefully it's because they're trying to figure out what's really being said. They've learned over time how to spot those wonderful phrases that don't always mean what they say. They have to search out the meaning. That's called "reading between the lines"—you leap over the credits and move right into the first act. I must admit that some writers think otherwise; they give you the truth right off. You've got to admire these people even if they don't show any warmth toward you. It's right for the sun not to shine too brightly in this country; the people seem to fit the climate. And perhaps it's not without reason that God gave them four distinct seasons. They want things to be precise, machine-like—they want to feel in control. Reading between the lines has become a habit; they're like gardeners who must have everything in neat little rows. However, they don't like to plaster the truth in public places, and, as a result, they keep it tucked away.

They've traveled through every country and crossed every ocean, but Jerusalem remains a vivid memory for them. And to think it happened so long ago! They felt compelled to race off to Jerusalem to rescue Christ's tomb. The Son of God wanted to teach us an important lesson: He let Himself be crucified by His enemies. Who were His enemies? People for whom the idea of love and brotherhood was anathema. Jesus asked us all to take off our masks so that the cat and the mouse, the hunter and the deer could live together in peace. The hunters threw their guns into the air and, as they caught them, shouted, "But how are we going to live?" The Son of God said, "The birds don't sow seeds and yet they eat, and the flowers—why, they're better dressed than you are." They didn't let Him finish what He had to say. But Christ kept preaching the idea of brotherhood. He kept telling his disciples, "Love one another." He knew how important this was—for you, for me, for everyone. This wonderful God, full of grace and goodness, this

Divine Lamb should have had disciples who were as stubborn on this point as He was. He had always told them to turn the other cheek. But they no longer knew which cheek to turn after both had been slapped. And He was no longer there to solve the problem. He had gone up to heaven. His tomb remained empty, and worse, fell into the hands of Turkish infidels. If Christ Himself had been in the tomb and had started to chastise them, they could have said to Him, "But where were you when we needed you?" And with clear conscience they could have walked away, saying, "Let Him deal with the Turks, who won't understand a thing he says." But since Christ's tomb was empty, they had to rescue it from the hands of infidels. This was the beginning of that long, elaborate movement known as the Crusades. The straightforward, fiery Parisians were once again at the point of battle—in fact, they were the leaders of this religious war. But did God plan for the Turks to capture the tomb so they too could feel the spirit of Christ? All of Europe thought otherwise, and the people kept on saying, "God wouldn't plan a miracle without us; it's forbidden." And so, as if to take the initiative away from God and beat Him to the punch, the people set off on the road toward Jerusalem, deliriously happy. Their past, present, and future sins were pardoned, especially those still to come, for, since the enterprise was led by a saint, and therefore blessed, the people were blessed also. After all, does the blood of an infidel have any value? If today Christians think it does, others still consider it tainted. "God wills it," they say, as if to wash their hands of the whole business. By nature people are greedy; they want their share of the booty, their share of the glory. They think their lords have enough of their own.

Yes, Jerusalem was taken, but at the price of a terrible slaughter on both sides. The Turks, who were determined to annex the Holy Places, dug in their heels and fought long and hard against the Crusaders, who were equally determined to colonize the area and eliminate the competition. Paris lost its most blessed king during those wars. But time has passed, and in so doing it has pulled the mask off the story that was the Crusades, revealing them for what they truly were. The people once again had been misled. Their real aims were hidden under the guise of rescuing Christ's tomb.

"The Turks threaten the entire Eastern Roman empire. They've taken over all of Asia Minor and have cut off the trade routes from the East to the West." The Byzantine emperor Alexis shrewdly called all Europe to his aid, citing the horrors that would result if the Turks were to take Constantinople. To further set their spirits ablaze and raise up their hearts, the Italian colonists all along the coastline of Asia Minor and Palestine joined him in recounting the atrocities of the Turks. They related terrifying stories of what the Christians were forced to endure. And they mentioned Christ's tomb to buttress their argument.

Alexis? Byzantium? To most of Europe these names meant little. But who wouldn't go and rescue the Holy Sepulchre? And so, once again, the beliefs of a whole group of people were exploited, much as they are today. The Templars, priests as well as warriors, played an important role in these Crusades. Their powerful order may have commanded respect, but they were scarcely loved, given their fabulous wealth.

Afterward, the Parisians knew all sorts of misery: restrictions from above and below, advances, retreats . . . For centuries freedom slipped through their hands. But not one single time did they become discouraged. They've earned the right to have the word printed in big letters at the top of every document, on the front of every building, for, in every century, there are always those who'd like to sweep this inalienable right under the rug. Thus, not only would it be wrong to criticize these people, it would be equally wrong to say they take things for granted. And so, with legs crossed, they sit and smoke their cigarettes, waiting for the metro. As sure of their city as they are of themselves, they get on, take a seat, open the newspaper, then get off, all without ever looking up. They have a sixth sense when it comes to the metro; every stop, every transfer is done by instinct. They're born with it. It's best to let yourself be carried along by the current. If you try to walk, you become an obstacle. Their looks tell you so. Your heels feel it, your shoulders too. They may say, "Excuse me," but what they're really saying is, "Get out of my way. I'm late." Long faces everywhere. The corridors aren't designed to make people smile; they're the battle lines you follow daily, the trenches you take to the front. There's plenty of light and air, and occasionally you hear someone playing the flute or accordion. And now and then you see a cripple. You keep running so that you won't end up like him; after all, you want to enjoy your old age. That whole underground scene could leave you with a bad impression if it weren't for the lovers. They try frantically to avoid the commotion around them, fanning love's flames by kissing in full view of everyone. You're constantly being reminded of the old saying that lovers are a world apart. And I must admit they do teach us how important it is to truly live each day. One thing's for sure: Paris is alive, and love is a part of everything she does.

When you meet a woman, etiquette demands that she be the first to extend her hand. But most of them are content to merely nod their heads. Then again, you never quite know what sort of woman you're dealing with. The married ones, of course, have wedding rings, but sometimes they take malicious delight in not wearing them or in wearing gloves instead. Women! Everywhere they're the same! What scenes they'd have caused if you hadn't given them a ring; yet, once they have one, they seem embarrassed by it. In this they're very much like the women back home.

As you know, when God created man, He baked him in an oven. The whites escaped as soon as the fire started, and the others followed as the temperature climbed. As if to prove to God that He had created real men, we were the only ones who braved the heat until He Himself felt that we had withstood the test long enough. Thus I'd always believed that whites are basically cold creatures. But I've learned otherwise. They're kind, warmhearted—even tender. We've got to remember not to judge on appearance or skin color. Let's face it, the women here must be warmhearted since they smile all the time. Just look at how much time they spend putting on lipstick; they want to make even brighter their already-bright white teeth. I'm so used to this now that a woman without lipstick always seems so pale, as if she's ill or something. The women here are so aware of the toll time takes on them that they spend every moment they can repairing the damage. They may not fool us with their makeup, but they sure want to fool time. They'll do anything to discourage it, to tame and finally master it. But is there anything in the world more patient, more hardheaded or cruel than time? The women know the answer, and that's why they do the goose-step on their faces—they're in a race with time.

Women know very well that what people love about them is often a certain particular detail: the way they walk, for example, the shape of their nose or, perhaps, a dimple. It might even be the way they look at you or how they hold their head. The married men here have become so smart that whenever their wives take off on a rage, they still manage to love that particular something about them—that nose or that dimple.

Paris, my friend, Paris! What can I say? Even an idiot couldn't hang himself in this city, for every precaution imaginable has been devised to prevent the possibility of anything like that happening. Paris is dazzling, to be sure, but the only thing that's dazzled me to the point of dizziness has been the metro. I smile when I see the number of tourists climbing up the Eiffel Tower or the Arch of Triumph, when I see those rich-looking people staying at the most expensive hotels. When they leave, every single one of them will leave with a particular image of the city in mind: that of a monument, a cabaret or other nightspot, perhaps, or the persistent memory of some special person. And what will I remember most? The metro. You've definitely got to be a bonafide African to remember the metro above all else. To me, that enormous underground spiderweb which lures everyone is the perfect symbol of all those who built the marvels we're forever admiring but who are lost in the pages of history. They worked by the sweat of their brows, but their names never manage to appear on a monument. And yet, they're what fame and glory are built on; because of them we're able to do what we do. But who even thinks of the metro when they're at work or with someone special? Who even thinks of saying that a machine is growing old, that it's dying and needs to be replaced? What's important is the fact that the metro's there, and on time. If we're able to stroll along the boulevards and enjoy the scenery, it's because the metro gets up before dawn and sleeps only in the wee hours of the morning. This network of corridors and escalators, ascents and descents is one big jumble of lines stretching to every corner of the city. And it's when you're inside those corridors that you become most aware of the enormous love the Parisians have for what their machines have given them: the opportunity to play king. Machines do the work and have given the people the right to be lazy and enjoy life, the right to steal a bit of time, even from tomorrow. But you've got to stay alert. You can't afford to be distracted or taken by surprise—the metro doesn't wait.

It feels good to be a part of something, and the metro is definitely a part of the Parisians. They're always saying, "I've got to catch my metro." Even though trains come one right after the other at any given station, you see people race toward the one pulling in at the moment. It's always a contest, and the first to arrive is the winner. If you see people hurrying along on the sidewalks, it's because they've got to catch "their metro." The funny thing is, no one ever gets hurt; no one ever gets caught in the crush. You see every sort of person here—except, of course, the Cadillac class—and everyone keeps their distance. In fact, they're as unto themselves as they can be. Some may be called Pierre, others Paul, but the similarities stop there. No two faces are alike. They can sit on the same bench and not exchange a word. Not even their color brings them together. But it's the same back home. That's why the elders were careful to put their respective tribal marks on their faces—so they could recognize each other. The face itself became an identity card. There seems to be no meeting ground here between those who use the metro and those who own Cadillacs. They might as well be completely separate classes; the former live in relatively poor areas, the latter in expensive ones. How different this is from what we do; at home, we rub shoulders with everyone, no matter how much money he has. How can you possibly live together without bumping into your neighbors, without knowing their names, without understanding what they're about or even visiting them? But we'd better not criticize them too much; it might be contagious. Here you associate by class. They inherited this custom from the Gauls, who for sure must have had a chicken for an emblem—after all, don't we use the term "French hen?" They're a people of protocol. They adore hierarchies and formalities, and their gods have always wanted gold . . . and more gold. They're always hungry for more and more and more! For some reason, these people who've made such a point of having the chicken as a totem keep slaughtering thousands upon thousands of them. The boulevards are filled with rotisseries, and in every one of them you find beautiful golden chickens turning on a spit. As you watch them turning, sizzling on the fire, you can understand why people would want to honor them; your mouth starts watering . . . you're swept away with desire. But I can also appreciate why some Parisians forget all about their totem. They can't resist the sweet, firm meat, even though it costs a lot. And yet in Paris you can also find palm cabbage. So far I haven't seen any palm seeds or palm wine, but I'm sure you can find them someplace or the other since the Parisians have found a way to bring everything else here: plants, herbs, animals, insects—foreigners. Everyone is drawn to this city; she commands the same attention a beautiful woman does.

During rush hours, crowds of people storm the metro, pushing and shoving their way toward the tracks. A train comes, the doors open, and the cars literally inhale the people. With people jammed together like sardines, the doors close; the train leaves. Promiscuity is a big problem here, and that's why some people refuse to take the metro.

Right next to me are two men dressed in black. They didn't even have to climb on—the crowd just swept them forward. Both work for God; one is a priest, the other a pastor. They say nothing. In fact, no one says anything; it seems to be a rule all abide by. Everyone stares straight ahead. As if continuing the protest launched by the Reformation, the pastor wears his collar backward, and the priest, ready for a fight should one come, wears a belt around his waist. Apparently this way of dressing has become a habit with them. For centuries now, they've both been fighting for Christianity, and yet, since they still harbor ill feelings for each other, they make sure they don't dress alike. The priest speaks to God in Latin; the pastor in English. Catholic churches are filled with flowers and beautiful gold work and elaborate statues all lit up with candles; Protestant churches are cold and bare. The priest willingly hears confession so as to absolve people of their sins; the pastor, on the other hand, refuses to do so, leaving that special function to God himself. Even Christ finds Himself split between these two men. His doctrine of love and brotherhood, as practiced by these respective ministers, reveals itself in the zeal with which each shows himself a worthy son of God. And that zeal has earned each of them a following. God's enormous patience proves that He understands everything—Latin and English—and that He sees everything and even knows our inner-most thoughts. He especially knows that a man's mouth, heart, and head aren't always in agreement with what comes out of that mouth. But how could you ask a Protestant to quit protesting when protests flood the pages of newspapers and magazines? Why, protesting proves that you're alive, that you pay close attention to what's going on. And to confound matters even more, what divides those two ministers of God—those two sheperds who are in charge of feeding us, divine sheep that we are—bears the name of a saint, Saint Bartholomew. No one's been able to tell me which side he was on.

What sort of devil was it that divided these two men of God? The fire was lit and the battle started when a certain Gutenberg invented the printing press. We don't even know for sure where he was born since so many towns claim the honor, but every one of those towns is proud to state they gave birth to the person through whom the devil continues to spread discord and anger. Our ancestors never ever quarreled over those venerable ghosts of the past, but today it's a different story. Village after village fights for the honor of having an important person's grave nearby. The amount of attention we give to those who've died, the importance we attach to them, given our habit of honoring the dead more than we do the living—all this still amazes me!

And so, it happened. Gutenberg allowed the Bible to be printed. This holy book, filled as it is with the words of Jesus, fell from the hands of priests into those of the people. Christ should have said that He hadn't come to bring peace but to sow fire. When the Bible was printed, however, the kings in Germany were still on good terms with the pope, the supreme chief of the Church.

The Bible quickly became bedside reading for every German. It sparked fire in their souls—so much so, in fact, that everyone began to ask questions. They soon rose up in protest against the whole matter of indulgences. A certain Luther, the leader of his clan, even dared to defy the one person all disturbed souls could look to for help—the pope himself. But Luther couldn't go and see him because the pope had issued a papal bull excommunicating him. Luther burned the paper, and this signaled his complete break with the Church. Part of the population sided with Luther against the pope; part sided with the pope against Luther. Inasmuch as Jesus had said to render unto Caesar that which is Caesar's, those who were associated with the protest were given the name "Protestant" in order to certify the fact that they were the first to protest. It's obvious the two ministers next to me have taken the protest even to the metro, guided as it probably is by someone who doubts that God ever existed in the first place. We're all a bit like this; we all have prejudices we can't always control. The world's made up of so many separate clans that there's no room for a person who isn't narrow-minded, who doesn't wear blinders. I wonder if we're truly helping to make the world a better place when we transfer to our children the prejudices our parents gave us.

These Parisians are a curious people to watch; in fact, everything here is worth watching, contemplating—providing, of course, you have the time, that you're constantly on the alert. But given this whirlwind we find ourselves in, do we ever have the time it takes to form honest conclusions about what we see? One must live, yes, but nowhere here do you feel that special fire that makes life worth living, that special something that creates lasting memories. You learn, of course, but you don't truly feel. Well, I'm a tourist, so I must keep running. I've found that Paris speaks to your eyes, not to your heart or your soul. And yet the city does have a heart and soul; she does have a spirit all her own. A young girl's face pressed against a window has a language all its own; so do the caged birds trying their best to sing, the woman selling newspapers of every political persuasion, the florist with dreams in her eyes, the painter working outdoors, the tugboat puff-puffing its lungs out—all this is Paris, and it all speaks to you.

It's said that faith moves mountains. Here it's crowned with beautiful towers and blessed with equally beautiful cathedrals. Some people in this city like to call themselves atheists. Come now, who're they kidding? We, who're convinced that He exists even if His overzealous priests tend sometimes to distort His image? Given the fact that their ancestors built these superb cathedrals, that their grandparents breathed the incense, and that they themselves have had their days regulated by the sound of bells since birth—it seems to me it would be awfully difficult to reject such a weighty past. You may not believe in God, but, given your origins, given your culture, you're Christian nonetheless. Notre-Dame and Sacre-Coeur may be monuments, but they're also part of your heritage.

It wasn't a Parisian who killed the Son of God. I wonder, however, what welcome we would have given Him if He had come to disturb our digestion by telling us to "give unto others," to discard our gold and silver, to leave our parents, friends, wives, and children and become fishers of men like Him. Fishers of what? Of men? I doubt if He'd have lived thirty-three years! Can you imagine, a young man who was born in a stable speaking to us that way? Giving us such advice? Us, with our heritage? After all, weren't we there when He was born? What would He do with our gray hair? Our fame? Our wisdom?

Whether blond or brunette, the Parisians resemble us as much as anyone. It's customary for them to spend most of their time in cafes, all of which are the very model of cleanliness. While the manager makes sure everyone is doing his job, one young man polishes silverware, another wipes glasses. They willingly, and politely, show you the urinal if you need to "hit the woods" or "make a landing," but on your way back, you'd better tip them for their courtesy. It's here, in the cafes, where you find the real Paris. I wonder why the Parisians don't all go by the name of Raphael. But the very fact that they refuse to use the name testifies to their wit and strength of character. Since the firm Saint-Raphael[2] seems to have a monopoly on advertising space—its name is printed everywhere: on benches, throughout the metro—the Parisians stay clear of using it as a name, even though they consume it.

I keep thinking about this as I make my way to the metro exit, pushed and prodded along as I am by a crowd of people anxious to leave the underground. But you don't love Paris if you don't love the metro. The city breathes, coughs, vomits and swallows, resists and rebels through the metro; the metro is at once its mouth, its lungs, arteries, veins, and heart.

2. Saint-Raphael is the name of a quinine aperitif.

THE AMOUNT of salt used in this country is frightening. Back home we tease the Baoulé[1] for liking salty food, but the Baoulé can't hold a candle to the Parisians on this score. And the tragic thing is, the Parisians have no idea just how much they use; they'd even walk through fire before saying one salt is better than another. Well, let them; they've done it so many times before it's become a habit. They don't even feel the heat anymore. They use it in all their sauces, and God knows there're so many different kinds that you can't help wondering if the Parisians rack their brains to keep coming up with new ones. You find it everywhere—on tables, in proverbs, and on baptismal fonts, where a priest dabs a little on the tongue of an infant newly admitted into God's fold. By doing this the priest reminds people that they are, in the words of the Creator, the "salt of the earth." The Parisians have never forgotten this. And when they want to enliven a conversation, they throw in a grain of salt. Ah! So that's the secret! If a conversation's flagging a bit and just can't get off the ground, let a Parisian approach, and suddenly it's alive and going strong. He simply has to appear and rub his two hands together for a conversation to start off again on the right foot, for it to acquire a certain style and importance, a certain charm and elegance, sparkle and wit. Parisians don't like things too dense and heavy; they prefer things light and airy, like lace. A foreigner stands there with his mouth open, wondering, How can they carry on a conversation so well and not let the other get a word in edgewise? But he forgets the Parisians' secret: the grain of salt. And you never know where they hide it. In their mouths? Their heads? They never talk about it; they pretend to ignore the magical effects of that grain of salt they carry with them everywhere. I tried using some. But mine simply melted in my mouth, and I couldn't rise to the occasion. My conversation was anything but brilliant. Nothing is worse for a Parisian who's out of practice and a bit dull around the edges than not to be able to attract a listener. It's an even greater disaster than that which befell Napoleon at Waterloo. But doesn't everyone have his own Waterloo?

1. The Baoulé inhabit the savannah region of the Ivory Coast between the N'zi and the Bandama rivers.

Granted, the location might vary; it might be a cafe, a living room, or a bed. But even in terrain like this, you're always battered and defeated, even if you thought everything would go like clockwork. You start out having faith in your words and feelings, and then along comes one little gesture, one little look, and the words won't come; the fire dies. These are ordinary, everyday occurrences, to be sure, ones that shouldn't mean a thing if people would remember their duty as "the salt of the earth": that is, to add a little spice to everything. Even then, however, the Parisians would still have their secrets, and they would guard them jealously so as to remain the one indispensable grain of salt.

Some say that the Parisians are getting tired of dispersing their grains of salt, that charitable acts like this threaten to get the best of them. I doubt it; all you have to do is watch them walk, watch how they accost you. They fear for us because they think we haven't the ironlike constitution it takes to live in Paris. They're so solicitous of foreigners that whenever they invite you to have a drink with them, they won't touch their glass until they've said, "To your health!" What they're really saying is, "I wish you good health in your journey through Paris." The only thing the Parisians want is for you to know their city up one end and down another—like a connoisseur, if you will.

I've never heard them say *"Tchin! Tchin!"* when they make a toast. The expression just isn't known here, at least not yet. On this point, the Parisians are way behind us, so far behind that they'll never catch up. It's about time we had a word or two more than they! Whenever a Parisian says, "To your health!," I respond with *"Tchin! Tchin!"* He looks a bit startled; but, too polite to say anything, he simply bats his eyelids, puts his glass down, and takes up the conversation where it left off, saying, "Now where was I?" As you can see, *"Tchin! Tchin!"* unnerves the Parisians. Well, as I see it, that's a point for our side! What could be nicer! . . . What am I hearing from the table next to ours? Two customers are raising their glasses and saying *"Tchin! Tchin!"* They must have spent time in our country. But there're many such travelers; many have brought the expression back with them. I know because I keep hearing it. I no longer feel as though I'm forced to endure the Scottish mists when it comes to making friends with these people. But they do everything they can to ignore me, and this gets frustrating after a while. They no longer look at us as though we were some sort of curiosity piece; nor do they even touch our skin to see if the color comes off. They do nothing, my friend, absolutely nothing! But I refuse to withdraw; I refuse to give up. I just keep right on running like the

Parisians, who don't even notice me since I too am doing what they're doing. In sum, I'm adapting—more or less. When someone pushes me, I push too—that way, we all make progress. It's certainly the only way to maneuver around the city during rush hour. The rising tide of humanity on the sidewalks and in the streets makes navigation almost impossible. You have to twist this way, slip through that way, and move sideways—anything to keep going. Utterly exhausted from all these acrobatics, you enter a cafe to catch your breath. That way you can enjoy the show from a spectator's point of view. Everyone here walks as though they're going to a fire; you make way for them or else . . .

These people, who lead such a full and happy life, willingly agree to abandon everything to serve their country. They call it the "blood tax." Some, however, fulfill their military obligation in an office. Wherever they're assigned, never ask them to beg off serving—they'll think you're a coward. They don't like war, but they happily pay the blood tax, just as their ancestors did.

From their Frankish ancestors they inherited one absolutely essential quality: speaking bluntly. Despite the fact that they love beating around the bush, in certain situations they go right to the point and say exactly what they're thinking. Ever since their ancestors, way back when, began worshipping mistletoe, they've kept the habit of touching wood to ward off evil. "Knock on wood!" they shout, and you see them touch a table, even if it's made of iron. Keeping the tradition alive is what's important. Yes, all this is part of Paris too.

I'm now at Notre-Dame, a place where Parisians gather together to worship God. It's the largest of their cathedrals, and an architectural marvel. For centuries people have engraved their faith in its stones. To give you an idea of just how big this cathedral is, try to imagine the two hundred years it took to build. What a people! They're full of contradictions! One moment they're looking at their watch, running to catch a bus, clattering down the steps of a metro station, stopping briefly to say hello to a friend rushing toward them—in sum, racing after time, which they translate, convert, and concretize into acts and words; the next moment, these very same people, with unbelievable patience and an out-and-out contempt for time, take two hundred years to build a house for their god. This God must be extremely proud of them. Our own God need not delay; if He wishes such a house, we'll seek his help in building one. After all, He's God; our duty is to regard Him as such and to thank Him every morning and evening and every time He helps us escape danger. We know we can do nothing without His help, and that's why we're constantly saying, "If God wishes, I'll do this or that." Would today's Parisians undertake such a work? They put their God aside, relying instead on their own heads and arms to accomplish something, and often they have to begin the same thing over again at least ten times. They're a stubborn sort, but tenacious all the same. As I look at this cathedral with its two towers rising eighty-nine meters skyward, I can't help but think of the enormous skill such a feat required, especially during a time when there were no elaborate machines. Three levels, no less! An absolute marvel! And everything about it speaks to you—every worn gray stone, where kings once walked, where the ghosts of the past mingle with the tourists of today . . .

It's a popular belief here that when our world is no more, God will leave His tomb and deliver His final verdict. They call it the "Last Judgment." I can understand why the Parisians are faithful, but I also understand why they sometimes revolt. Ever since they were seven years old, they've heard nothing but talk of the devil, of hell; because of this, many end up believing that God is cruel. And they don't hide the fact anymore that they're fed up with such talk. Usually when they say this, they're at their wits' end. You can't get them to budge an inch; whatever you say is nothing more than hot air, and hot air doesn't always fill sails. Let's not forget that these people are descended from a race of boatmen, and they're accustomed to tracking the direction of the wind in order to catch it at the right moment. They've even reached the point where they picture heaven as a series of bottomless deeps rather than a fathomless hell. If, back home, we tug a bit at the ears of our gods and deprive them of dinner when they refuse to listen to reason or hear our troubles, the Parisians, on the other hand, light an enormous number of candles around the statues of saints. It's their way of trying to call attention to their prayers, of asking that their wishes at least be considered. But the Parisians are on earth, and in order to get the attention of the saints, who're in heaven, they have to toast them with candle flame.

Once the Last Judgment is given, the good people on God's right hand go to heaven, while the bad people on His left head for an eternal hell. This is enough to give one nightmares, to strangle any desire to live. It's enough to prevent you from saying what you want to say, from leaving your mark on the world. Unfortunately, the impression you're left with is that of an angry God, one with a whip in one hand, candy in the other—the same impression we have of the white man in our country: medals in one hand, a prison in the other. People have discriminated against God: they've made Him a God of war—albeit a holy war—instead of a God of peace. Your skin color and the amount of money you have speak louder than the voice of God within us. And "he who remains silent, gives his consent." Given all we do in His name, it's no wonder that God retreats behind a majestic shadow of silence. Isn't there any way to make God speak to us so that we all can be convinced of His existence? Will the Parisians ever know?

Opulence and luxury once reigned supreme in this church. Here resounded the voice of Bossuet who, in his eulogies, tried to convince royalty of God's true meaning. Despite the fact that all those who lived then are dead now, their descendants repeat the very same gestures—just as we repeat those of our ancestors. All generations have floundered in the same quagmire we call life. We want to believe we can change things, but our efforts are barely noticeable.

You've got to admire the Parisians, however, for telling their history as it is, for refusing to embellish even the tiniest detail. They maintain they're the descendants of a race of poor people who lived in meager huts. These people, who instinctively line up, who refuse to tolerate any gate-crashers, seem to be a walking history—a page right out of a long and glorious past. They know they represent something special; they know they play a definite, and indispensable, role in human affairs. And they want to tell the world about it. After all, didn't they capture the Bastille and, in doing so, tell the world that even kings could fall? Didn't they tame the spirits of the Seine, build a series of canals, and thereby civilize the river? And now they've covered the river with ferryboats carrying tourists and lovers. Each day they try to make their city a bit more beautiful.

They want to be adored, and that's why they love to see their city decked out in all her finery. There's no city in the world more attractive, more romantic than Paris when, at twilight time, she dons her jewels for a grand parade. She becomes an absolute coquette! No matter in which direction you look, the city is like an elegant elder statesman who wants to charm the young women nearby. Every quarter has its own special character, its own distinct features. The inhabitants can change their makeup, but the neighborhoods remain true to their original nature. And they'll do anything and everything to stay that way. There's a fashionable quarter, a middle-class quarter, and a poor quarter. You recognize them by their restaurants and hotels, and by the way the young people behave. These quarters—actually twenty-two separate villages—are called *arrondissements,* and they're inhabited by people who don't speak to each other. This is quite the opposite of what happens back home when a stranger arrives in our midst. We're all informed of the event right away, and off we go, from concession to concession, cracking jokes over the fence to show that there're no barriers between us. For sure we have our little quarrels, but by the next morning we're friends again, and we show our joy by sharing a glass of liqueur. Everyone swears to have forgotten even what started the dispute, and the sun continues its course—how well it knows us humans! It knows that tomorrow it will rise to another such reunion, to another such series of sworn statements. But back to the point: in our villages everyone knows each other. There's nothing of that here. It just so happened that I had to shout to get the attention of a friend of mine, and you'd think I'd committed a felony! At least everyone looked at me as though I had. It's okay to make noise, but shouting's forbidden. Shouting's permitted only in the bush; but this is Paris, and Paris is civilized. The only cry the Parisians tolerate from a person is the same one you hear when a fire truck goes by: "Help!" They realize that someone in extreme danger has no other choice but to scream. I pity the Parisians on this point; it seems they're so caught up in what's proper and what's not that they don't have time to truly live. They're so on guard they've even managed to tame their hearts by chaining them to a leash. Having done so, they can say they've mastered their passions—something they love to brag about!

Can you imagine this? A heart on a leash? And yet they're absolutely astonished when they have to admit that their hearts don't always obey them, that sometimes they follow their hearts. But the meaning of this escapes them. Once they've decided to control their hearts, they consider them controlled. So be it. To act otherwise is to lose face. And the Parisians would rather lose anything except face. Thus, they follow in the illustrious footsteps of that exalted king who, at the conclusion of a disastrous battle, once said, "All is lost save honor!"

People here could live twenty years in the same hotel, have their door right next to someone else's, take the same elevator, and still not know each other. All live in a world unto themselves; they mind their own business and demand the same of others. This attitude is the direct result of the respect each Parisian accords the other and the inviolable right they each feel they have to live the way they want. That's why the world seems to stop at the threshold of certain dwellings. You could be dressed all in gold, and the Parisian would look at you in the same way he looks at beggars who happen by. Your car could be a hundred meters long, and he'd smile at your extravagance rather than your good fortune. If you decided to appear naked, he'd think you had your reasons, even if you left those reasons at home. You can live the way you want to in Paris, unless, of course, you're like those stars that need other stars to shine. Because they seized control of a prison and cut the head off a king who thought he was God on earth, Parisians aren't surprised by anything. As a result, the city lacks a certain warmth. I now understand why there're so many lovers. Nowhere else in the world can you feel more alone, and nowhere else does everything around you—the gardens at twilight, the indifference of the people passing by—elicit such strong emotions. Paris can be deadly for those who're alone: that's why you see so many couples out walking with their arms around each other; that's why you see so many friends banding together in groups. Single men and women just don't seem as happy; they seem disengaged. One thing is certain: to be in Paris and not to be loved is a veritable catastrophe. But the Parisians love to be self-sufficient. They want their families to be self-sufficient, their friendships, too, and their politics. Of these, the most important is politics. They can go a week without seeing a parent or a friend, but they can't go a day without reading the newspaper that reflects their own political persuasion. You see them buying *"L'Humanité," "L'Aurore," "Le Figaro," "France-soir,"* or *"Le Monde."* To buy your adversary's paper would be tantamount to bringing grist to someone else's mill or beating yourself with someone else's rod. And so, every day every Parisian steels himself against the arrows and claws of his adversary. Granted, here they don't have their arrows and claws lined up ready to attack, since they tell themselves their civilization is superior to ours; they simply accumulate them and put them in storage. Cannons first—save the arrows! The Parisians, you see, voluntarily set themselves restrictions so they can better defend themselves in the future.

Is it bad for a country to have so many different points of view? It's the only way they can remain true to themselves, the only way they can avoid being swept away by others. Given the absolute whirlwind of ideas you have here, it's easy to see why they want to attach themselves to a particular buoy, to a particular paper. We can't ignore the fact that Paris is a world unto itself, a veritable ocean in which you can drown if you don't know how to swim. And many are the Parisians who know how to swim, who know how to burn what they worshipped yesterday in order to adore that which they burned today. But in this domain, the Parisians aren't always the smartest, even if they know how to suffer a defeat and still come out smelling like a rose. Back home we have what we call "bottle men," those talented souls who put the same corks in all bottles, whatever their shape or size. Just look around you. Who doesn't want to climb the ladder of success? Who doesn't want to be hoisted above the crowd and held up as a model? Thus, we keep floating, like corks, accepting everything. It seems we become more civil that way.

The Parisians are so discreet they don't even know who's sitting at the table next to theirs. They have a thousand reasons why they choose to live the way they do, why they choose to keep to themselves. But Paris isn't made for solitude; it's made for human companionship.

The women here have everything that's needed to warm you up, whether or not they have the right figure, but they're wary of men and treat them as mere commodities. They're always on the go, so it's difficult to grab hold of them. But even if you were to catch them, you couldn't hold them for long because they adore playing tricks. Everything hinges on the way you approach them; start down the wrong path just once, and you're through! How do you learn this? The women tell you. But how do you find a good woman? Don't misunderstand me, my friend, I mean exactly what I say!

As is true back home, here too love doesn't reside in words, but in acts. In fact, words are so lacking that when Parisians want to break off a relationship, they simply say, "It's over!" We do the same thing. But how can a people with such a full, rich language deign to use such an old expression? Matters of the heart are the same everywhere: it's difficult to strangle our feelings, to cast them aside; and this is true whether you pretend to be civilized or actually are.

Paris has infected its women with a strange disease. They're constantly looking in windows and mirrors, constantly arranging their hair. I even find myself peeking over my shoulder to see if my hair looks okay! They're determined to be up-to-date, in the right color and style, and the only concern they have is how to cover up their wrinkles, how to keep looking young. As part of this effort, they support their breasts by enclosing them in brassieres, and when they pass by you they leave behind a trailing scent of perfume. But they're especially dangerous in the way they walk. It's designed deliberately to bother you, to make you want to launch after them. Ever since they've been free to marry whomever they want or to divorce if they so choose, they've had a horror of chains, even of necklaces, whether they're made of pearls or not. In fact, it's rare indeed to see a woman wearing a necklace since almost all of them have become, you might say, "free of the leash."

The first thing Parisian women do when they enter a restaurant is to look at themselves in a mirror; then they light a cigarette and open their newspaper. They too want to stay informed since they know that men always try their best to control their every thought. When they're through eating, they wipe their mouths, freshen their makeup, move the table so they can get out, and then leave, without so much as glancing at anyone; or if they do happen to glance at someone, it's done so discreetly that you rarely even notice. In our country, we'd say they have "the eye of a fox." But they're far from being the sly and cunning creatures foxes are; if they don't look at someone, it's because they don't know them. That's the way they're brought up. Like the men, the women only consume one glass of wine when they eat. But their manner of drinking is strange indeed. They majestically raise the glass to their mouth, but their lips barely even graze the edge before they put the glass down again. And they eat without opening their mouths! If I hadn't seen their teeth before, I'd think they were toothless, for they eat just like our toothless people do back home.

They have many different ways of arranging their hair. Some pull it back in a ponytail; some knot it up in a twist; others let it hang down on their shoulders; and still others have it cut short like a man's. And they use all sorts of different products to keep their hair looking the way it does. You often see them heading for a beauty parlor, where they're put under what look like enormous white pots. Moreover, here men do women's hair. Yes, I agree, it's a strange country! You could encounter twenty Parisian women; they could all look alike and have the very same eyes; but no two would be dressed alike, nor would they have the same hairstyle. Even more disturbing is the fact that not only would you have twenty different hairstyles but twenty different hair colors. Younger women wear tight-fitting dresses that mold to the shape of their bodies, and because they do they're forced to hop like sparrows when they walk. You can't take your eyes off them, and it's often a struggle to remember to behave properly. Yes, Parisian women are free-spirited, and I'm convinced that their way of dressing, of revealing their necks and the small of their backs, of displaying their firm bodies is all designed to attract a man's attention. And what man isn't an artist? What man doesn't love art for art's sake?

The women I've seen in restaurants and cafes all pay their own checks, unless they're with their husbands or fathers. Given the fact that they're used to paying their own way, you'd think they wouldn't let themselves be ordered around, unless, of course, they're madly in love. But such madness is short-lived because they always return to their senses; they always remember their rights, the fact that they're free. It doesn't cost much to sustain a friendship with a woman here, since, by mutual agreement, gift-giving is no longer required. You can, if you wish, get her something for her birthday or take her to the theater, but she won't complain or resent you if you don't buy her a gift. She knows she has your love, and that love means more to her than gifts. If she feels you care for her, that you understand her, she's happy enough. And there's no doubt you'll be well paid in return—that is, she won't fail to turn up when you've arranged to meet somewhere. Even more, the skies of Paris will always seem sunny to you. But don't ever think that Parisian women forget their vested interests. The other day at noon I overheard a woman shout at her husband, "Enough now! Let me speak!" I fully agree—men don't have exclusive speaking rights. But those who think they do make fun of women by saying they're nothing more than chatterboxes. Chatterboxes or not, women intend to speak, and speak they will. Yet when they speak to their husbands, they gaze off into the distance so as to avoid eye contact. They raise their shoulders, breathe deeply, and smile. I wonder what they're looking for—the ideal husband?

Every Parisian woman emits waves, which you must know how to capture. It's a matter of recognizing them. Many times a friend has nudged my elbow and said, "Hey, she's looking at you."

"Who?"

"Oops, too late."

"How did you know she was looking at me?"

"Just wait. In time you'll know."

I don't think I'll ever know. Their smiles are quick to appear, but they fade just as fast. And their eyes keep slipping away. You never know how to detain them, how to approach them, much less how to make them stay interested. Like our women, they want you to fire them up so they can watch you pine away slowly as they fan old memories.

The Parisians have a strange way of showing their love. They sit side by side, smiling, looking deep into each others' eyes. All of a sudden the woman will close her eyes, as if to collect her wits or get her bearings. You see her shake her head. The man responds, "But yes! But yes!" Again they look at each other, and their smiles become even brighter. The man puts his hand on hers, and she begins to breathe deeply. She crosses her legs, pulls down her skirt as if to barricade herself, and they kiss. They kiss each other on the mouth, on the hair, neck and eyes. There follows a moment of respite, and the woman, yielding to her feelings of the moment, trustingly rests her head on the man's shoulder. He holds her around the waist and caresses her hand. Suddenly, you'll see her shudder, sigh, then close her eyes again. Parisians kissing are a part of the scenery here; this too adds to the city's charm.

You can't believe the women's eyes, my friend! They're huge, round eyes that laugh and sing one moment, show tenderness or scorn the next, tease and question you the next. They avoid me, though; perhaps they don't understand my language. All I know is that when they do look at you, they seem to be looking off into the distance. Since they're so used to being attacked, maybe they're scanning the area to make sure they're not taken by surprise.

The women's stockings are so sheer that you can see the veins on their legs. Given the fact they're the color of skin, it's hard to tell at first glance if a woman is wearing them or not. To be sure, you've got to look at the back of the leg, to see if there's a seam. I'm positive this wicked little detail hasn't escaped the attention of those who make them; in fact, right now they're probably figuring out a way to eliminate it. If that happens, they'll have created a perfect illusion. The older women cover their faces with a veil and prefer to dress in black. I confess to having been impressed with the black uniforms of waiters and waitresses when I first arrived, and my first day here I thought these women were all in mourning. But the color black becomes them . . . I must also confess to being rather bitter that there's no place in their hearts for that same color—my color.

Parisian women also have these charming little phrases they use with their men friends; the most common one is "my cabbage"—a highly prized vegetable in this country, I might add. The men say "my darling" or "my dear." Every one of these expressions is said in such a loving way that you see them shoot straight to the heart. And yes, my friend, these women have gorgeous mouths! Painted as they are, they look like ripe berries that need to be picked fast, before your neighbor does. You want to scrunch them between your teeth to test how firm and sweet they are. I now understand why the young men want to press them hard, take them all in, and savor their flavor, even in front of a whole group of people. And the women have such a provocative way of passing their tongues over their lips when they lower their eyes or open them very wide. I should leave this country now! One of these days, I may find I can no longer be an impartial observer, that I lose utter control. But what I'm afraid of most is being swept up in this whirlwind, thrown out of my usual gear. Already, I find myself taking little sips when I drink, having an espresso at appointed hours, and no longer shouting to get the attention of a friend; I even find myself instinctively lining up, reading my newspaper, arguing with passing motorists, and wearing a raincoat. These are definite signs of my evolution, of my assimilation. But I don't have a girlfriend yet. And I'd love to have one right now . . . Maybe I'll race outside, grab one, and, in plain view of everyone, kiss her passionately—just as the Parisians do! Maybe then I'd get rid of all my anxieties. Maybe then I'd shake these feelings of prejudice and be truly free . . .

Did I say that Parisian women don't let themselves look at anyone for long? I was wrong, my friend, very wrong! Two women have just thrown veritable harpoons my way, and they managed to hit me right in the heart. I've been bitten, my friend, no doubt about it. I find myself following them, walking like an automaton. Wait . . . What's going on? Where are they? I'm convinced there're sirens living among the women here—just like the sirens back home who cause you to lose your mind as soon as you see them. I'll wager that those who just disappeared have long hair tumbling over their shoulders, the eyes of a sorceress, and milky-white skin.

Jealousy has got to be the most virulent disease in this country. But this isn't surprising. With such gorgeous women around, you have no choice but to keep your eyes open, really open. And Parisian men open theirs so wide that one day they won't be able to close them again. According to their own statistics, six thousand attempted murders occur every year; of these, one thousand actually do take place. And there are two thousand suicides. Apparently jealousy is to blame for many of these. You can see the horrible effect it has on families. The disease is most rampant in October, right after vacation, when everyone is busy harvesting their crops. It's at this time of the year that people worry the most about money.

Normally used to showing their love with flowers, Parisian men now appear with pistols in their pockets.

"Do you love me, my darling?"

"Yes, my cabbage."

"Swear thay you love me, my little chicken."

"I swear, my sweet."

As soon as she has sworn, a powder of a more explosive nature has its say. And it hits its mark. In times past, when flowers carried the day, juries were a bit more lenient. Even though their verdicts were occasionally rather severe, they'd try to soften the blow with flowers. But we're in another age; things mechanical rule today. Have we lost the ability to understand the language of flowers? Have the sounds of guns going off affected our hearing? I'm sure that's what makes flowers shake their heads all the time. It's clear they regret losing those days when people had time to spare, when people truly knew how to live, how to love. We can go ahead and put them on tables and windowsills; we can put them in store windows but they know they've fallen from grace. We scarcely have time to smell them anymore, to admire their beauty, or hear what they're saying. Yes, people keep buying them, but they no longer understand their special language. I keep wondering if this century will ever be able to retrieve their meaning. We keep plowing the earth for its riches; our factories keep flooding the market with goods we don't need in a perennial attempt to outstrip our competitors; we keep trying to get people to march to a certain beat—that of the second hand on a watch. For what? Meanwhile, civilization continues to lose its once-eloquent voice. It's been reduced to nothing more than a series of peeps and squawks.

In the cafes, however, Parisian women chatter away in their usual melodious fashion, each one trying to outdo the other. Periodically you'll hear one of them say, "Are you listening, my dear?" Now and then you suddenly see them raise their arms, clasp their hands together, roll their eyes, and cry out, "Why that's impossible! It can't be!"

When you see the Parisians alone, man or woman, you realize just how much they're in control of things. All hell could be breaking loose, but there they are, sitting in a cafe, quietly reading their newspaper or writing a letter. A waiter could be whirling a tray full of glasses over their heads, and you might be wondering if he's going to drop it right on top of them—but they seem oblivious to it all. They just keep right on reading or writing. The waiter, meanwhile, just slips away, smiling. Noise? What noise? They spend their lives in noise. In fact, they'd probably die if, all of a sudden, there were no noise.

Cafes and restaurants are the only places where Parisians willingly consent to waste time. The waiters, however, have none to spare. As soon as you enter a restaurant, for example, the maitre d' comes over to take your order. You've got to keep signaling the waiter, who, in turn, merely says, "It's coming, sir, it's coming." The waiter is something of a philosopher, you see. You might refuse to relax, but he's making sure you do. In this way, he forces the customers to relinquish their machine-like ways; he allows them to rediscover their humanness so they can enjoy the meal and the lovely surroundings. He wants them to delight in being among people again, to want to reach out to others so they can forget their worries for a while. But do we realize what a waiter's doing? Do we really know why he makes us wait?

The women, most of whom have that awful habit of eating without opening their mouths, do open them when they're calling a waiter. It's one of the miracles wrought by restaurants. They know full well that, by speaking softly, they won't be easily understood, that you'll be forced to go over to them to hear what they're saying. Not only does this permit you to hear them, it also means that you'll be held captive by their perfume, by their warm smiles and fetching looks.

IF WE ENTRUST to the spirits the protection of our villages, here the Parisians give that job to a special type of soldier, one who wields enormous power. No one does or says anything without first thinking of them. They're called journalists. Moreover, they're an unruly sort with rather obscure origins. From what information I can lay my hands on, they seem to have descended from a powerful tribe called writers—people of insatiable curiosity and incredible audacity when it comes to writing what they think. They're considered a bit lazy because they do no manual labor at all, preferring instead to work with their heads. And their heads work so hard and churn up so much that they always seem feverish. These journalists act as censors and assume the right to speak out on anything. They can destroy a person or praise him to the skies—it all depends on the mood they find themselves in at the moment. But they're not like the town criers we have back home, nor are they people who beat out messages on drums. Given their mysterious nature, it's more accurate to equate them with gods, since one small article they write might stir up more noise than eight drummers gone wild. Whenever they decide to take matters in their own hands, their pens are never at rest. They go at it full force—like wildfire. And the fires they start never die out. You could be doing nothing more than changing addresses, a job, or your name—whatever, you'll feel yourself burned but good. For sure, memories are made for remembering. And what's nicer to remember than what your neighbors do? They may seem sweet, easygoing people on the surface, but underneath they adore gossip, they adore prying into another's affairs—and, as a result, distorting the facts—and they keep their mouths shut when it behooves them to do so. After all, maybe some of them are members of the secret police. Who knows? Before a politician signs anything, he first thinks of that race of wasp-masons who, with a mere flutter of their wings, can topple an entire political system. Yes, we have our various spirits; here they have journalists! And we all live in fear since we never know what they're planning to do next. If something piques their interest, out come their stingers. If, on the other hand, nothing does, they maintain a prodigious silence. Should you find yourself in their good graces, they'll cover you in flowers, but if your views conflict with theirs, they'll strip you naked. If only they stopped there! But no, they'll push the matter as far as they can, even seeing to it that your photo makes it to the front page. After that, no matter where you find yourself, people will be pointing fingers at you. They'll yank you out of the shadows and expose you to the full glare of the sun. "Here, readers, here he is, in his true colors!" Like the spirits back home, they can make or break you.

Their true ancestors, at least the true ancestors of all writers, are the minstrels, who in turn gave birth to the jongleurs—people who, with a hurdy-gurdy slung over their shoulders (a type of primitive guitar), could be found in public squares, in knights' castles, at village crossroads, before the gates of churches and monasteries, and at fairs and market-places, reciting from memory not only works others had written but their own compositions as well.

Since it was their custom to travel around the countryside, to go wherever their fancy led them, they lived outside the law; thus, they had no civil rights whatsoever. They had no home. And so, they were forced to live on the margin of society. Was this simply because they had no roof over their heads, no hearth to call home? I wonder . . . After all, of what value were people who merely sang for their money? Neither the peasants nor the townspeople had the least regard for them. The former didn't like them because they weren't peasants. What good were people who didn't know how to work hard, who knew nothing about harvesting crops, who, especially, ignored the saying "Good Friday's frost means bread and wine are lost."

The other professions regarded them in the same way, since they too considered those perennial vagabonds nothing more than charlatans, mountebanks, and cheats. However, their chief character trait—the one that's lasted throughout time—is that of never agreeing with each other. While some pulled one way, others pulled another; but there was also a third category, a group of those who mocked the entire world, who made everyone a scapegoat. As a result, you never knew which of the three groups was right. Each could mount solid arguments for why it believed the way it did, and you could find yourself leaning toward one camp or another. Now, what they want more than anything is not so much for you to feel their sting but for you to be on their side. Once they feel you're with them, they'll see to the rest—and with the loudest voice possible. I've never heard it said that they rig elections; if that were so, the dead and those absent would vote too. But the dead wouldn't even think of venturing forth on election day here; they'd be afraid someone would indeed change their vote.

Quick to speak, these jongleurs, whose imaginations are as fertile as those of our own storytellers, love more than anything else to harangue the newly rich, whom they call "thieves." Dazzled by their newfound wealth, these people make fools of themselves trying to impress their neighbors. I've come to realize that Johnny-come-latelies are the same the world over, and I find that the term "thief" fits them like a glove. Not simply because they want to lord it over their neighbors but also because, in "borrowing" the habits and manners of another class, they try to be something they aren't. I sit here wondering, however, what I would do if, tomorrow, one of these new-age minstrels decided to call me a thief. How could I fight back? After all, I too wear tails sometimes; even more, I've been known to kiss ladies' hands and drape myself in the Napoleonic Code. In some sense, then, I too am a thief, albeit neither the old-money nor the new-money kind. But, let's face it, there's no reward for those who aren't one or the other. My, how times have changed!

Those jongleurs of times past never lost their bearings as they went from hamlet to hamlet. One place was particularly special to them, a town called Arras, which they considered their capital. There, a miracle was performed in their honor. Once again, it was shown that God had created people, not noblemen, commoners, or other such stratifications. Money, birthright, and position did indeed breed such differentiations, but in His eyes they meant nothing. The Blessed Virgin Mary was to give feudal society, replete as it was with the constraints of hierarchy—as is our own world today—a stiff lesson in equality. She was to show that rich or poor, nobleman or commoner, soldier, priest, or minstrel—whatever—all people were God's children. The story goes that somewhere up north there were two jongleurs who were enemies. Although their wanderings took them in completely different directions, one night they both had the very same vision. The Blessed Virgin ordered each of them to go to Arras and present himself to Bishop Lambert and to tell the bishop what she had revealed to them: that the lepers who threatened to take over the town would be cured of their illness. They arrived at the town on the appointed day, but the bishop didn't believe their story—bishops, you know, are wont to doubt. You can imagine his astonishment when, after the jongleurs found themselves friends again, he saw our sweet Mother herself, dressed in her blue robe and white veil, holding out to him a flaming candle whose burning-hot wax fell into a cup from which the lepers would drink and be cured. This is what's known as the "miracle of Saint Chandalle of Arras."

Perhaps this is merely a charming story illustrating the fact that jongleurs should lead us toward the light. I do know that ever since then they've kept the torch held high and have managed to light upon all fronts, just like soldiers. Spreading information is indeed their priestly mission. A fire isn't started anywhere that they don't come running. Not many of them die in their beds during such times, for they find restraint too heavy a load to bear.

Every jongleur had a master. And when the master felt that his student was ready to test his own wings, he'd call the jongleur in one evening and give him his blessing—much as our parents do when we're ready to set off on a long voyage or about to undertake a difficult assignment. It's important to realize that traveling wasn't easy then. Cutthroats lay in wait along every highway and byway. This was true for us too and it gave rise to the proverb "When you leave for Tiassalé, you don't ask if there're bandits en route." You knew there were. You knew that you'd have to go through bush and through deep dark forests where they operated. You knew you'd have to follow the same paths they did. That's why we traveled in armed groups. Bandits weren't lacking along the major routes either. Their activities became so well known that here, people without scruples, who conduct themselves like bandits, are called "Cartouche"[1]—after the most famous bandit of them all. For twelve long years Cartouche and his gang roamed the city and outskirts of Paris. They were a veritable scourge, and, unfortunately, their race isn't extinct yet. Today's disciples, however, rob banks in broad daylight. The way they figure it, the more they take, the more they won't need—good Cartesian reasoning as I see it. In this country, if people save money, they do so for their old age, when, let's face it, they don't have the energy to enjoy it. Everyone here lives and works for their old age, and they're so good at economizing that I've yet to see a bread crumb make its way into a garbage can. Nothing's thrown away, and if by chance something is, you can bet it's of absolutely no use anymore. The Parisians even recycle factory smoke and sewage. They feel obliged to do so. This, I can understand. Since everyone lives for himself and doesn't want to have to depend on another, they take every precaution they can so as not to end up destitute. We'll have to adopt

1. Cartouche, properly Louis Dominique Bourgnignon (c. 1693–1721), was the head of a Parisian band of robbers. *Chambers Biographical Dictionary,* rev. ed., J. O. Thorne, ed. (New York: St. Martin's Press, 1968), 234. Hereafter referred to as CBD.

the Parisian way of economizing if we ever hope to take control of the situation we find ourselves in. In fact, economizing is so much a part of everyone's life here, that merchants see to it that you're never gifted a cent. If a cent were given to fifty customers each day, that would be fifty cents; fifty cents every day for a month would equal fifteen dollars; and fifteen dollars every month for a year would be one hundred and eighty dollars. Merchants know this. They know exactly what the amount would be in ten years and what they couldn't buy if that amount were missing. Typically Parisian. They never leave anything to chance, nor do they follow to the letter what's in vogue because that would put considerable strain on their pocketbooks. It's not a point of honor with them to change clothes twice a day to show how much money they have. That's why you'll never see their closets stuffed with suits and dresses and shoes. <u>Such excess embarrasses them</u>. They'll do all they can, however, to save for their old age and to see to it that their children are well educated, for it's a good education that allows them to climb the social ladder.

Life, for us, is something that must be lived and enjoyed today. We mustn't neglect the future, to be sure, but it's important to concentrate on the present, since families as we once knew them are on the brink of disappearing. Perhaps we're to be held responsible for this. If this does indeed happen, should we consider it bad or good? I, for one, don't dare make a definite pronouncement since I'm convinced each of us will have a say in the matter in the future. Who knows, maybe families are stronger now because they have more money. But it's clear that what we used to mean by "family" has collapsed, since we no longer share our children with our relatives; instead we prefer to raise them totally by ourselves. We're all for our own kids, but we could care less about our nieces and nephews. Given the difficulties we face today in terms of educating them, we risk adopting another's customs, of becoming strangers to our own past, and this threat won't disappear until we find an answer to this agonizing problem. The entire issue's enough to strangle us, and we must do some serious thinking about it—and soon. But we can't let ourselves get carried away with trying to explain why we've delayed in acting so long, nor can we keep blaming the schools for no longer teaching the important moral and ethical values. There's no time for that. What we must do immediately is take a stand on the matter, roll up our sleeves, and get busy constructing a new society, one that safeguards the warm community of yesterday and at the same time deals with the actual concerns of a modern civilized nation. We were born in a world that is now out-of-date, one, however, that continues to want us to move slowly. It's still convinced that crawling along inch by inch is the only way to create something lasting, the only way to evolve and progress. Are people born conformists? Can we really say that the child born in Paris this morning will simply continue in the footsteps of those who, for two thousand years, have moved cautiously? That child will hesitate before doing so, and that's what makes it civilized, "Parisian" civilized. We too could have been born in Paris; we too could have inherited all those values acquired and accumulated over the years. And society would have given us everything we needed to continue our education, to improve ourselves. But what would have happened to our own values? Would they have been able to resist colliding? How could we have given them the strength they needed? You can't help but think about all this when you're here; in fact, Paris forces you to think. The city has faced one invasion after another, one occupation after another, and yet she's still the same Paris. Somewhere, somehow she's always managed to find the strength of character she needed to weather whatever storm came her way.

admiration

We have a good example here of a people determined to remain true to themselves. The tramp you see is a Parisian tramp; that is, he's different from other tramps you encounter. The boats on the Seine are tied up in a way our boats aren't. The fishermen stand differently from ours; even the trees have their own way of bending over the river. The Parisians wouldn't change their city's face, her habits, or conduct for anything in the world. Her rhythm is that of the people who inhabit her, and thus it will remain. The clock atop the prison beats out the same time, and no one even notices except for the tourists who live on the margin of the city, even if they stay in the most luxurious hotels. Paris is like a woman who, when attacked, will surrender her body in order to save her heart and soul.

Well, we're a long way from those oddball journalists I was talking about earlier. They'll for sure unsettle any feelings of complacency you might have and do their best to make a nonconformist of you. To return to our jongleurs . . . a master would say to his student:

Go, my child, and sing of the noble deeds of yesteryear to those who wish to imitate those gallant acts. Let the ancients be the models and, along with them, you yourself and what you've created and learned from the study of French history. If they like what they hear and are enlightened by it, they'll reward you; if, however, they choose to remain stingy despite your appeals to their generosity, go deep into your cave and hide the treasure whose beauty and luster aren't appreciated by the people of today. In time there will be those who will admire them, and they will raise altars to the unknown minstrel. Your body will feel the sword-point, but your spirit will live forever in heaven. Go, my child, go to the courts, the halls of government, and the towns and scatter to the winds your songs of bravery and heroism to give hope to those living in misery. But remember, your only gratification will come from within.

Marvelous, indeed, are those heroic deeds of the past, not to mention the enormous sacrifices that characterized a jongleur's life. Even the words of advice given by the master are worth repeating. Don't you agree? Especially when we consider the fact that a jongleur's life was a thankless one, much as it continues to be for us back home. They had to hang on, even if it meant dying for what they believed; they had to make sure the torch was passed on, that the wonderful words of the writers they recited would continue to live. A jongleur's life here, however, was more exciting. In Paris there were noblemen who listened to them; where we come from, however, the privileged ones wouldn't consider stooping so low. And the young people are in too much of a hurry to waste their time in such a way. Part of the fascination Paris holds for people, part of its charm comes precisely from the fact that artists and poets are considered special. The Parisians have refused to treat them as mere stumbling blocks on the margin of society. Everything here breathes poetry. Even the smallest stone houses the soul of a poet. And every lawn, every garden is a veritable poem in itself. We mustn't, of course, forget the flowers—true jewels promenading their beautiful colors throughout the city. Who else but those with the soul of a jongleur, of a poet or an artist could love these flowers? Paris, my friend, is filled with such souls. And as long as they exist, the city will never die. Never! For even under the barest of walls there's a bit of ivy growing, the soul of a poet pushing through once again.

"Gratification comes from within." The master's words seem truer for us back home than elsewhere, however. They denote a profound understanding of humanity and encourage the jongleur to continue playing the role he was born to play. People who were invested with a mission, who knew of their inherent value, even if they were, for a time, misunderstood—indeed underrated—could never be sweet, easygoing people. They were at the mercy of their fantasies, much like modern-day journalists in their search for truth.

It's easy to see that beneath every momentous event in this country lurks a journalist. Every government coddles them while waiting patiently for the opportune moment when they can shut them up in order to teach them that accommodations must be made on earth as well as in heaven; that before they open their mouths to speak, before they begin writing, they should listen to the wisdom of the proverb that says to chew over what you're going to say seven times before you say it and to dip your pen in ink at least ten times before committing words to paper. But these journalists could care less about prudence and proverbs, and it's a fact that prisons don't frighten them in the least. They want justice, and justice they will have. The example most often cited is that of a certain Zola, who pursued his love for truth as far as to say that, even for reasons of national security, you can't condemn an innocent man. At that time, the country was divided into two camps, journalists included. It was finally Zola who won the battle, because he had truth on his side. Another writer, Victor Hugo, exiled himself, and from his own island rock shot arrows at an all-powerful emperor who had wrenched his government from the path it should have followed. And they're many more examples besides these. Yes, even in the most absolute regimes, journalists have continued to write, to criticize. Guardians of liberty, priests in the service of human dignity, they have, by their sacrifices, made Paris a city everyone would love to live in, because here you breathe freely, you feel at ease. One by one, they've managed to rescue our rights and freedoms from kings, emperors, and dictators, the same rights and freedoms we enjoy today and that make life worth living. We love Paris because here, far more than back home, we can say what we think, even to the head of the war department. People here feel they're worth something, and they never forget that. The Paris of minstrels and their descendants is, however, a city built from blood and full of dreams yet to be realized. This you know by the way the people talk. I now know why we've developed the detestable habit of watching every move the Parisians who visit us make. You can't be from Paris without, at the same time, being a light in the dark that still reigns in our country. Every Parisian tourist is fully aware of the continuing mission of his country to enlighten the world, to track down the injustices and see to it that men everywhere are freed from all vile forms of servitude, from all those who wish to suffocate them. Thus, by her very vocation, Paris welcomes to her bosom all the disinherited of the earth.

We love Paris because very few rights exist for us back home—or, if they exist, we know them by another name. We love Paris because, far away from all forms of suffocation we can feel ourselves open up. Then again, perhaps it's because we're looking for a kinder world. Who knows? But maybe we should follow the example set by the Parisians, so that we can one day install a similar climate back home, one whose memory will always remain with us . . . Oh yes, I forgot to tell you that given the age and the mania people had for differentiating themselves from each other, jongleurs appeared in all sorts of various guises: singers, composers, poets, writers, journalists—and many others I don't have time to list. Whichever they were, they were all critics, and they all loved to travel. . . .

At the beginning, they were a rather mysterious people since their place in society wasn't clearly defined—just as we are today, because people only want us for our strong backs and our resources. Little by little they were finally able to enter the once-famous salons run by women who had a different view of them. These women exerted considerable influence over the poets and writers of the time. In fact, they acknowledged them as their own. What I'm saying is that here too women take charge—but discreetly so. If, one day, we arrive at the point where we imitate the Parisians, the first thing we'll do is emancipate the women and give them the same right to move freely. Without them, nothing permanent could be accomplished. This is a well-known truth, but it doesn't hurt to keep shouting it from every rooftop.

These salons go back to the time of the Crusades, when men left their wives and daughters at home. While they waited for their husbands and fathers to return, minstrels entertained them by praising their beauty and speaking of knightly deeds. In time, the salon was established, and the women proceeded to polish the manners of the otherwise unmannerly men—husbands, lovers, brothers, and writers. Certainly Tallemant des Reaux,[2] one of the most famous writers, owed his best work to a woman, the Marquise de Rambouillet. Another writer, an abbot, in a reversal of roles, confessed, "Women of quality have definitely polished my manners and nourished my spirit." No one, however, has been able to give me the name of this abbot. All those I've asked have politely skirted the issue and deftly steered the conversation in

2. Tallemant des Reaux (c. 1619–1700), was a French writer, born at La Rochelle; he married his cousin Elizabeth Rambouillet, whose fortune allowed him to devote himself entirely to letters and society. His famous "Historiettes" (written 1657–59) are illustrative anecdotes rather than biographies. Admitted to the French Academy in 1666. CBD, 1246.

another direction. The Parisians have the marvelous ability to play deaf when they're confronted with an embarrassing question. To them, such questions are impertinent and ill-timed. One wonders if there are certain areas in their history they'd prefer to leave a bit hazy, or if they simply don't want to fan an argument that's not quite dead yet, since they have in their possession a powerful firebrand that goes by the name "Baranger's Law," or "the law of the Wild West," which is often invoked when people threaten to come to blows. The name itself is enough to make people even more obstinate. Baranger must have been a real scoundrel for his name to be called up by those on both sides of an argument. Underneath, he probably wouldn't have hurt a fly, but for some his name means war. Let's face it, there are people who meet with this sort of fate. After all, wasn't the Divine Lamb changed into a lion after its death? God keeps waiting for the prodigal son. Now it's our turn to go and look for him, and when we find him, we'll point right in his face and say, "If you dare move an inch!" . . .

God won't wait forever for the troublemakers of the world to quit playing the renegade and join up with the others who sing His praise. I think we'd all agree He's waited long enough, but we also know that He must continue to curb His anger.

THROUGH THE intervention of women, then, writers gained stature in a world where it became a mark of good taste to know and appreciate literary works. Such appreciation, however, still maintained many of its feudal qualities—that is, it surrounded itself with large castles, drawbridges, communal ovens, and common people in the service of noblemen. What really explains the admiration for writers, what made them appear "civilized," was that they were considered somewhat like servants, like storytellers whose duty it was to praise the master and his family, to stand up for his interests, and defend his politics. You hear it said that certain journalists continue to harbor this sort of mentality when they charge off to defend powerful interest groups. Just because they no longer journey to Arras doesn't mean they've lost their bearings, for even in serving the powerful they still find time to take up more sensitive subjects, for example, rape—or, to use their phrase, "the treatment of women." Thousands of women in Paris have simply vanished. And, as you know, back home there's also talk of the same thing happening. Some say that truck drivers and fishermen are acting in collusion; all I know is that we don't dare go beyond a certain district at night for fear of encountering an absolute jungle. If, given their usual audacity, the Parisians feel free to speak out against the disappearance of young women, where we live everything's hushed up. The whole situation could be solved, but it would be like pouring hot coals on an open wound.

To know, appreciate, and love a people, you must study their history, and the longer I study that of the Parisians, the more I realize how much their ancestors resembled ours. The Parisians would like to argue the point, but they won't, not because it just might be true, but because I seem to be taking them backward, forgetting in one fell swoop the thousands and thousands of years of hard work they've put in to get where they are now, forgetting, too, the place they've carved out for themselves in the world. They'd probably like to smack me over the head, but it's already been abused and mistreated for years—two thousand years to be exact. Why, it's enough to make me laugh! If they were as old as they think they are, their skin would have darkened with age. But they're barely even tan! There's no way in the world they can say they're the oldest people in the world, even if they think so. Their walls were white at the beginning and have become gray only over time. But how in the world have they managed to keep their skin white? Of course, the sun has continued to do its work since it has changed the color of some peoples' hair to brown. And who knows, maybe some day . . . No! We'd better not scare them! But even if that were to happen, the world would become the same all over, and that would spell death for us all, since it would destroy our efforts to take pride in our own color while, at the same time, acknowledging the value of another's.

If the men keep us at arm's length, it's because the women haven't yet granted us access to their hearts. They could, perhaps, let us approach their lips. But no . . . Those lips, which, as I've already told you are absolutely marvelous, are always painted with lipstick . . . And the men love to pluck kisses from them. They've obviously developed a taste for the color red but not for the color black. What, I ask you, would we do in their place? Do you really believe the women would wear black? Men see only lips, smiling lips beckoning them closer. . . . But let's not throw stones, since we're men too.

Proud of their birth, even if it resulted from an ordinary gestation period of nine months—the difference being that they were born in a castle under the kindly eyes of loving nursemaids—noblemen laughed at the impertinent bantering of those writer-servants, those madmen who had but recently arrived at the court. However, as soon as the arrows were sharpened, those very same noblemen didn't hesitate one minute before they began to treat them as mere servants, beating them at will. The rod's a sign of power, of authority; it's also used to punish shameful behavior. This is a country where extremes often find themselves shoulder to shoulder, and perhaps that's why blacks and whites tend to get along here. Kings carry a rod, but it's called a scepter; old people have what's called a cane; and great military generals who've earned the rank of field marshal carry a baton. Lawyers have their own symbol of authority, the president of the bar, and policemen carry theirs around with them in their belts. You've got to admit, in this country the rod has played a significant role.

Spiritual concerns have relinquished their rights to this city. People here feel perfectly free to race after money; their consciences don't seem to bother them at all. Back home, however, we keep to the shadows, to the wall side of the pavement. But this is a relatively new country. And new countries are places where spiritual matters have no place until all appetites have been satisfied. Investments are what matter.

Investments and profit. As you well know, the spirit can't invest, much less produce dividends. It's a flame, and no one likes a flame that doesn't give them something—either in their living rooms or in their souls.

The actual master of these modern-day jongleurs is a man by the name of Renaudot,[1] in whose name a prize is given. Even though numerous prizes exist to encourage writers to excel, the one most highly valued is the Renaudot. Why? Well, the Renaudot's the Renaudot, that's why. There's no other like it. Although the award given by the French Academy generates a lot of excitement, it'll never diminish the value of the Renaudot, which remains, you might say, the one true compass in the storm of daily life. Renaudot was a doctor of poor people, but he was also a man of action, a genius. It was he who launched the *Gazette,* the first newspaper. As Paris grew and grew, people needed a newspaper to keep them informed. In time, newspapers became a part of Paris, as important as the sparrows and monuments. Everybody remembers Renaudot. To show just how grateful we are for what he did, we should be calling all our children back home by his first name: Théophraste. Here, on the other hand, no one's called Théophraste because the name's no longer in style. Nowadays everyone goes by Marie-Chantal, Brigitte, or by other twentieth-century male and female saints' names. On the calendar there're even the names of saints who, like God, must be on holiday, since no one seems to pay any attention to them at all. They're too old-fashioned.

You can't help but be amazed to see how determined the Parisians are to keep abreast of the news, to stay informed. For them a day without a newspaper is a day lost. It's like missing the train. Worse yet, it means they can't hold their own in a conversation. Would that God would let such a thing happen to us! Maybe, then, we could better understand what's happening in our world! Maybe we'd stop being old fossils playacting the role of a modern man.

The "Sun King," Louis XIV, knew the awesome power of writers firsthand, and since he wanted to be known and remembered for the most brilliant reign imaginable, he invited many writers to join his court and saw to it that they were given an allowance. These writers sounded his glory throughout the realm and made sure everyone knew

---

1. Renaudot, Théophraste (1586–1653), was a French Protestant doctor, born at Loudon, who settled in Paris in 1624. In 1631 he founded the first French newspaper, the *Gazette de France.* CBD, 1073.

what earned him that glory. Given the fact that the king was earning more praise than the actual sun itself, every morning when the sun opened its eyes, it looked to see if the king, that is, the Sun King, had usurped its place in the sky. But the sun saw so much of what was going on below, that it simply continued its course across the sky, certain that it would outlive all ephemeral glories. It merely laughed when it saw people trying to outlast their appointed time on earth by erecting statues of themselves in the courtyards of marble palaces—statues that had no weatherproofing whatsoever! When his reputation was fully established and secure, he terminated the allowances of those writers he felt had become nothing more than parasites. Several, however, refused to accept their walking papers lying down. One of them, a man by the name of Ménage,[2] who had been particularly well provided for, said, "As for verses, I have none for this occasion; any praises sung now would not only sully the reputation of the poet but would also be suspect in the eyes of the public." This man should be held up as an example, for people like him place their love of truth, their freedom and independence above anything else! Ménage may belong to an age long past, but his words have survived time. Why is it we have such difficulty understanding them?

Alongside the official press, there developed a secret, clandestine one that appealed to the masses. This always happens when a group (or groups) of people feel their concerns are being ignored. The writing was done by people from all walks of life—lawyers, abbots, fruit vendors, and housekeepers, among others—and the paper profited from the very fact that so many were involved in its production and dissemination. These underground newswriters were considered evil by the official press, which wanted nothing more than to bring a halt to their activities and see them behind bars. Light under wraps, so to speak. But whether they were exiled, whipped, sentenced to hang, or forced to row in the galleys, nothing would stop their courage, their determination to say what they wanted to say, to see to it that all Parisians had the same rights. The same is true today. For them, nothing is worth more than freedom—the right not only to call themselves Parisians but to be

2. Ménage, Giles (1613–1692), was a French lexicographer, born at Angers, who gave up the bar for the church. But he spent his time mainly in literary pursuits. He founded, in opposition to the Academy, a salon, the Mercuriales, which gained him European fame and Molière's ridicule as Vadius in "Femmes Savantes." His chief work is his *Dictionnaire etymologique* (1650). CBD, 875.

Parisians, and to know that one of their kind sits in the town hall and fights for those rights. They want to see the flag waving over their heads too; they want to wake up and go to bed knowing their laws are secure, knowing also that they have the right to go to battle to make them better. Their whole attitude bespeaks these desires. Journalists seem to be the guardians of this freedom and wouldn't hesitate a minute to die for it. Ah, yes, my friend, the walls of Paris are gray from the gasping last breaths of the dead who helped make this city so grand, so modern.

PARISIANS ARE extremely logical in some ways; they know that the shortest distance between two points is a straight line. But they refuse to follow that path in certain situations because they find it too rough and steep, too filled with potential booby traps. Contrary to what we do, they never call an older man "Papa" or "Grandfather," preferring, instead, to simply call him "Mister." Thus, they put him on the same level as they do a younger man. And if an unmarried woman is sixty years old, they still call her "Miss," whereas back home we'd call her "Mama," or "Mother," even if she doesn't have any children. For us, age deserves special respect. Carried to the extreme, this passion for equality means that a descendant of the Sun King himself would have the same name (on paper) that the thief Mr. Dupuyht has. These people who'd never ever consent to put a man, much less a whole group of men, in chains, who scream to high hell when they see someone remaining hopelessly behind the times in matters involving national and international relations, who, in sum, are in the vanguard of progress, whose very land gave birth to human freedom—these very same people, my friend, hold firm to the opinion that one white person is worth two blacks. Given this, how could a white person possibly hold hands with a black, much less kiss him? How in the world can we stop being relegated to the back rooms of their hearts? I opened my eyes and took a long hard look at the women. I'm sure they found me impertinent, probably an insufferable boor too, but I had to behave that way so as to clarify certain issues for myself. They look like our women, and like ours, they cook, do the laundry, clean, work in the yard, rock their babies, love their husbands, sing when their hearts tell them to, curse when a vase falls, and become angry over nothing only to break into laughter the next minute. Moreover, like ours, they can't stand the thought of a rival. Some love a good fight; others, who know how to begin one but never how to end it, prefer right off to talk things over. Some even surrender their lips. A point in their favor. Others shout, "Hands off!" But they all have the same hand gestures when it comes to stopping a man's arm in midair, the same ability to withdraw when temperatures get too hot, and the same apprehensions when their partner breathes a bit too deeply.

90

Perhaps they inherited this prejudice from their ancestors, one that in time grew to include the whole range of a musical scale—no, several musical scales! Whatever, it's now the size of the largest edifice imaginable; and you couldn't begin to budge it, even if time and firsthand experience were to prove that whites and blacks have the same value, are made of the same stuff, the same clay, and are capable of showing the same belligerence, the same patience, the same light-hearted humor.

Although these people drink, eat, and read with their thumbs, they refuse to turn those same thumbs your way. They're always asking "How are you?" even if the face right before them looks troubled and would appreciate another form of questioning. They're always calling you "old chap," no matter how young you are, and punctuating every phrase with "ooh! la la!" to the point you think they'll never quit. They erect statues to all their great heroes and even to the Son of God, the Mother of God, and the adopted Father of the Son of God; and they paint them white for no valid reason, hoping thereby not only to gain the supreme blessings of heaven but to overtake us in the race for God's love. Moreover, they're forever beating their breasts, accusing themselves of committing both capital and venial sins. Everything here, you see, is classified, ticketed, and numbered. The people adore music so much that you see them stop whatever they're doing as soon as they hear the first notes of a violin. I tell you, they are the most superstitious, the most formal, the most tradition-bound people I've ever met.

No matter where they are—in hotels, restaurants, and stores, even on street corners where they find themselves face-to-face—Parisians indulge in a battle over who's the most courteous. It's as much a question of who will consent to pass first as it is a question of who will have the honor of letting the other pass first. When such encounters occur, they forget their watches, preferring instead to listen to the courtiers of days past, to their Gallic ancestors, whose blood continues to flow in their veins.

"After you, sir."

"Please, after you."

"Go ahead, sir."

"No, no, after you."

"You're too kind!"

"Please, I beg you . . ."

And they'll remain right where they are for minutes on end, each wanting the other to pass first. After all, it's the polite thing to do. But if it's a matter of who's first in line for the bus or the cinema, a fly couldn't squeeze between them, for as soon as they see you coming, they stick to each other like glue. The women, especially, don't like to give way since they're used to going first. Whenever a man meets a woman on a staircase, he immediately plasters himself against a wall. The woman thanks him with a smile and moves on. A woman whose path I crossed this morning charged on by without even giving me time to act as the other men do. She must think our women back home have nothing more to do than make babies, carry pots on their heads when they go from village to village, and cry when we die. This one didn't even smile, but I followed the rules and got out of the way anyhow. To be sure, the people here are difficult to figure out; I think they keep racing after time so as to keep ahead of us. We, however, choose to take our time; we like to rest periodically, especially since we've come such a long way. But even though we've dragged ourselves along beneath a sun that's darkened our skin, it isn't as though we've never seen anything! They too will have to slow down one day—after all, you can't keep running for centuries on end without resting. Granted, they do take vacations, but two weeks or a month simply aren't enough, given the type of life they lead.

Despite the fact that they resemble machines in both manner and pace, the Parisians have still managed to remain human since they haven't yet been able to raise even one of the veils hiding our destiny. They keep scanning the horizon for something that continues to elude us, and this gives us much to worry about. I was told about people here who're capable of raising the dead and conversing with them, who're also able to summon the devil and extract certain favors from him. Some, they tell me, might even be married to sirens who can provide them with fabulous fortunes since they have very powerful genies at their beck and call. But I can't confirm any of this, for I've yet to meet a single one of these people.

The origin of certain fortunes is due to persistent labor, to continual economizing, rather than the favors of a devil whose conditions would be draconian at best. You must realize that these people have a special fondness for preserving the strange and wondrous: for example, Pope Leo's *Handbook,* Solomon's collarbones, the *Secrets* of Albertus Magnus, and the pentagrams and prayers of Abbot Julius. Most notably, of course, they still believe in the special properties of the hazel tree, without which, they maintain, nothing can succeed. Both the black cat and a black chicken, along with perfume, play a paramount role here.

Not to mention fortune-tellers! Parisians love to pierce through all those mysteries that surround us from birth to death. Maybe they're secretly afraid of going to hell. Given their inquisitive nature and their love of good times, the women are the principal clients of the marabouts here. They do everything they can to force the hands of the gods, who, however, remain insensitive to their charms. After all, these women have so much to preserve, so much to maintain!

Paris too has its share of tragedy, and you find it hidden in palaces as well as slums. Every day hearts are broken, relationships dissolve, and illusions come tumbling down. More than one man or woman you meet has just received a new wound, but their sense of propriety forbids them from showing either the new hurts or the old ones. Some would like to leave Paris and be born again under another's skies—ours, for example. They yearn to quit the rat race and break free of all constraints. Their solitude weighs heavy on them, and as they march to the established beat they dream of faraway places. I saw one of their marabouts once, one of their fortune-tellers. Dressed in a white shirt, he wore a little goatee and dragged his house around with him, like a snail. He was an impressive sort, with nice fat cheeks. Let's face it, the credulity of some has always brought life to others. The authorities have given him special testimonials, and he has those affixed to his house on wheels. This proves that people in high places value his profession for what it is. These testimonials also help keep people on the right track; that is, they help them dream of better days tomorrow. I should add that this fortune-teller operates in full daylight in public. It's become almost a game here to try and predict the future. Rats, mice, pieces of string, knucklebones, shells—they're all part of the machinery. All you have to do is give them your first and last name and date of birth. Back home we wouldn't be required to give this information. In fact, the last thing we worry about is the precise date of our birth. All we need to know is how old we are and we can say in a flash how long we have to live. What are a hundred years in the general stream of things? We are born, we live, and we die. Why do we need to worry about months and years? It makes no difference whether we're worth anything or not; death greets us all. Indeed, life is one continuous fatality. It's better just to keep going without worrying about how long you've been on this earth. But the chief concern of the Parisian is to keep track of everything, to literally succumb to time's dictates and make sure you leave your mark. The most striking example of this is the number of monuments and tombstones you find in cemeteries here.

When we die, we join the seasons in their eternal cycle; we become part of the water and the wind. We leave no trace except in our loved ones' memory. But here they leave elaborately carved marble tombs, as if to say to Father Time, to Death, "See, you can't defeat me!" But Time is deaf from birth and understands none of the earth's languages; it merely continues to nibble at the fingers of statues and break tombs as it rushes to destroy everything. It seems, then, that whenever you visit a fortune-teller's house on wheels, you do nothing more than trust your left hand to one made of iron.

The Parisians believe there's an enormous difference between the right hand and the left hand, so much so, in fact, that when the politicians gather together, those on the right represent an opinion diametrically opposed to that held by the people on the left. They forget that one hand needs the other—that the left hand washes the right one and vice versa. One is absolutely nothing without the other. But for them, right is right, and left is left. Period. With your hand extended, the fortune-teller starts pushing buttons that allow him to converse with his mechanical spirits. The spirits move into action. They consult with each other as their blue and green eyes buzz and blink on and off. One of them suddenly cries out, and everything comes to a halt. Immediately, a piece of paper and a small medal appear, and the man, smiling as though he knows the gods' innermost secrets, hands them to you. You pay in advance in order to avoid what both the man and the spirits abhor: any form of dispute or annoying discussion. But what if the spirits have made a mistake? The client waves his arms in protest, but the spirits in the machine remain silent. The fortune-teller himself, however, is used to such adversities and has at his disposal more than one slick phrase to help him out of a sticky situation. And they seem to work. After all, the fortune-teller elicits a certain confidence; his goatee is so white, he's so open and honest-looking that the client simply accepts what he has to say. It's up to the gods to correct the error. Then again, perhaps the client was too abrupt in extending his hand, too cruel, and the spirits thought he was trying to offend them. But perhaps they considered him a bit too namby-pamby about the whole thing and wanted to conclude their business with him fast. I wanted to try. However, I didn't know my date of birth, much less the hour and second. Couldn't the gods tell me? They reveal everything except that, since they assume everyone knows when they were born and will never forget it. If they saw to it that you were born on such and such a day, at such and such an hour, then it's up to you, and no one else, to remember. As a result, I wasn't able to communicate with the mechanical spirits of the old man with the white goatee.

"I'm sorry, sir, I absolutely must have your date of birth. Without it I could make a mistake."

"But I'll give you my first and last name."

"That won't suffice. I need at least the day and the month. You know the stars—why at any moment they can shift location."

I've concluded that our own genies are stronger than theirs. Back home all we need to do is present ourselves, knock on the door, and grease the palm of the interpreter so that the gods will talk.

Like us, Parisians believe in dreams. However, they want to make sure they keep this belief in its proper perspective and under control, for the last thing they want is for anyone to point a finger at them. Cartesian to the end—that's their motto, no matter the situation! But periodically, and in quick succession, they can cite numerous examples of famous dreams experienced by kings, archbishops, and other fine gentlemen: Henry IV and Louis XIV, for example, even Napoleon I. They can even recall those of their saints, Saint Augustine in particular, one of the most venerated pillars of their church. Moreover, they attribute one of their most famous songs to a dream an illustrious composer had. One summer night, Joseph Tartini[1]—or so it is said—heard the devil playing a beautiful piece of music on a violin. He awakened and transcribed it, calling it the "Trillo del Diavolo." Such authoritative examples play an important role in furthering the Parisians' steadfast devotion to dreams, so much so, in fact, that they can exclaim most emphatically and succinctly, "Not all dreams are lies." The attention paid to dreams is so widespread here that newspapers even have a column entitled "Your Horoscope," in which someone analyzes the effects of the moon and stars on any given birthday. People here believe everyone was born under a star that is either good or bad; if you happened to have been born under a good one, you were simply lucky. Artists have even tried to influence their fate by calling themselves by the same name—"star"—clearly signifying their intention not only to

---

1. Tartini, Giuseppe (1692–1770), was an Italian composer who gave up the church and the law for music and fencing. Having secretly married the niece of the archbishop of Padua, he fled to Assisi. After living in Venice, Ancona, and Prague, he returned before 1728 to Padua. Considered one of the greatest violinists of all time, he was also an eminent composer, whose best-known work is the "Trillo del Diavolo." CBD, 1248.

place themselves above mere mortals but also to tap into the habit everyone has of looking up. As you know, for us a halo signifies the death of someone important; two rings, an important event in world affairs; stars that turn red, a catastrophe...Here, some people even claim they can read the stars. Kings have frequently consulted them before embarking on a major venture. Louis XI once had an astrologer predict a brilliant victory in an upcoming battle. The king happily set his forces in motion, only to end up defeated. Furious, he called for the astrologer, who spoke with such assurance that the king became very worried: "Sire, the heavens have just informed me that I will die three days before your majesty does." The king was so affected by this that he let him go. No one knows, however, which of the two died first.

The most famous of these astrologers was called Michael of Notre-Dame, better known as Nostradamus.[2] His predictions were taken as absolute authority and are still studied today. Whenever a major event seems to be brewing, people race back to his *Centuries* to try to make sense of it.

Parisians are so eager to know everything that they even have their palms analyzed—not to mention the bumps on their heads, the wrinkles on their faces, the way they walk and laugh, even the way they hold a cigarette, exhale the smoke, and yawn. They think the horseshoe and four-leaf clover have special qualities that bring happiness and good luck. The number thirteen, on the other hand, is considered a harbinger of evil. In this country you'll never find thirteen people at a table; if by chance you do, it's commonly thought that the thirteenth will die sometime that year. Restaurant owners have solved this problem by only having tables for one or two. There might be thirteen people in your party, but they'll sit at different tables. If someone sneezes—and etiquette demands that you hold your nose so you won't make any noise—the others joyfully shout "God bless you!," after which the one who sneezed must say "Thank you."

Many people have several first names, each of which, they believe, will intercede on their behalf when it comes time for them to meet

2. Nostradamus, or Michel de Notredame (1503–66), a French astrologer born at St. Rémy in Provence, became a doctor of medicine in 1529. He set himself up as a prophet in about 1547. His *Centuries* of predictions in rhymed quatrains (two collections, 1555–58) earned him a great reputation. Charles IX, on his accession, appointed him physician-in-ordinary. CBD, 951.

God. Yes, they're a very logical people, even though they refuse to walk under a ladder.

optinism

But underneath their hard exteriors, the Parisians are just like us, swept along by the winds of time to who knows what destination. They believe in heaven but fear death. Like us, they too look at their wives and children and friends and say to themselves, One day I must say good-bye to all these people I love, but for what? Where will I go? Sometimes they want life to end, but let a bird sing or the wind blow softly through the trees, let someone smile at them, and immediately hope revives and they enter into life's stream once again. They value friendship, honesty, and candor and respond warmly to a baby's smile. The same is true for us. They simply have different customs, that's all. The more I see, the more I realize that, fundamentally, little separates us. This is what I've been looking for ever since I arrived. Everywhere I go, I see people like us: talkative, shy, courageous . . . I watch them eat and drink, laugh, love, dream, converse, argue, run and stop running. And I've learned just how meaningless the barriers between us are, despite the fact that some continue to ride them like hobbyhorses.

Have I mentioned the subject of tipping?[3] Originally a tip meant wine for the valet or the waiter. You gave them wine for their services. But as time passed, instead of giving them a bit of nature's bounty, you gave them money. Thus, you no longer give them something to drink, but something to buy a drink with. Given this custom's long history, it's not surprising that the Parisians hold the practice in such high regard. But when I first arrived here, the whole matter of tipping came as a shock. I needed a place to stay. A taxi-driver spent the better part of an hour driving me from one hotel to another. When we finally stopped, he pushed a button on the meter, and I paid the fare as indicated.

"That's not all, sir."

"But that's what the meter shows."

"Yes, but the tip's not included."

I had to pay up since their laws demand that you do, but I find the whole procedure totally unwarranted. If I send for a messenger, I know I owe him a tip, but for a taxi-driver to demand one when it's his job to drive people around is incomprehensible. If a waiter tries his best to serve me right away, I don't mind giving him a tip, but if he makes me wait around and then, pen in hand, presents me a check with a percentage added in for a tip, I revolt. The Parisians, however, find this per-

---

3. The French word for "tip" is *pourboire* —literally, "to drink."

fectly normal. It's one of their customs . . . Yes, I ended up surrendering. After all, I'm in Paris; I must obey their laws.

And let me tell you about the wedding rings women wear! These small chains are made of gold, silver, or platinum, and the women wear them on their fourth finger where, it's said, a special vein leads directly to the heart. Women about to be married insist on having a ring, and they wear it as long as their love lasts. But if that love dies and a rupture occurs, they put it away, swearing never again to make the same mistake—a mistake they find themselves making, however, several days later. One kind look their way is enough to make them forget their precious oath. Yes, my friend, a woman's heart is made of soft-burning coals. Our own women are no exception.

In churches I've seen people make a special sign they call the sign of the cross. This dates back to when their newly founded religion was attacked on all fronts by older established ones that refused to allow themselves to be dethroned. Christians of that era, who'd already adopted the fish as a symbol of their God, followed by the Lamb, recognized each other by this special sign, which, in essence, means, We make the sign of the cross on our foreheads, over our hearts, and on our arms. When we make it on our foreheads, we must confess our sins to Jesus Christ; over our heart means that we'll forever love Him; on our arms signifies our duty to tirelessly perform His work on earth. For them as well as for us, the smallest of gestures carries the weight of centuries. We're all tied to the past whether we want to be or not—and that's another point we have in common.

On Bastille Day, July 14, a day that liberated the common man from the burdensome rule of the privileged class, the nation's chief, who's called the president of the Republic, makes a formal address, awards medals, and pardons certain offenses committed by civilians and military people alike. The origin of this ceremonial procedure is as follows:

Ever since Clovis was crowned king at Reims, all other French kings have been crowned there, because it was in Reims that the holy oil sent from heaven for the express purpose of annointing kings was preserved. After the king had been crowned, there was a celebration. Musicians performed on fifes and oboes, noblemen distributed money to the poor, and soldiers fired salvoes. Gunpowder settled over the festivities, and money went the way of all smoke. (I wonder if the people here can, in good conscience, complain about the heavy taxes they now pay when they consider the ease with which public monies are dispersed!) As part of the celebration, the new king set about freeing some of the prisoners. This is what the president of the Republic continues to do. I've been told that one day Paris will be the center of an empire whose entire population will be enslaved. I don't believe this. Granted, Paris has many enemies, but a city that introduced the world to the whole notion of human rights and human dignity—and saw fit to inscribe those ideas in bronze—to my mind wouldn't know how to bend a people under a yoke no matter how light that yoke might be.

The Parisians have an extraordinarily powerful secret word from which, they believe, their own power derives: "abracadabra." This word was handed down from the beginning of time, and they in turn have passed it on from generation to generation, as if they were obeying orders. The true sense of the word, however, is known by very few. For the most part, you only find it in those secret works of mystery and magic known as the occult, but the Parisians—people for whom two plus two equals four—use it to designate anything that defies logic.

Their kings were buried in a very special way. Contrary to even our earliest customs, there were no public sacrifices. Here's what I was told:

A chorus of voices was heard, and then the monks of Saint-Denis appeared, walking in double file. They would slowly make their way toward the abbey, where, in a room expressly designed to receive the dead, they would prepare the body for burial. There too, as was found in Reims during the coronation ceremony, a table and chair would be laid out for the king; but this time the scepter and sword of justice wouldn't be placed on the table, but near the coffin instead, on small squares of black velvet. The chair would remain empty. For eighteen days, according to custom, the table was covered with food. And each day a herald would repeat these words: "The King is served." A moment of silence would follow, and then the herald would say, "The King is dead."

When these eighteen days had passed, it was time for the burial. Once the funeral oration and the mass were completed, the coffin would be taken down to a vault. As it made its way toward its final resting place, the monks would follow along, reciting liturgical prayers, waving incense, and sprinkling holy water. Then, when the herald gave his call, all the royal insignia would be brought forth—the crown, scepter, and sword of justice—and they would be tossed into the open vault. There was one exception—the French flag. It would be lowered for a moment, to bid a final adieu to the dead king, and then raised immediately so as to show that the noble flag of France would never die. It's only at this moment that the king's death took on its official character.

Yesterday I watched a funeral procession pass by. Men dressed in black followed the hearse in their cars. Yes, my friend, they're always in a hurry, even when they accompany their dead. No one danced, and there were no long-winded sermons. The women didn't even cry. And no one fasted or shaved their heads. As soon as a death takes place, someone comes to clean and dress the body; others dig the grave. Crowds never gather as they do back home. No one even throws money for the passage from this world to the next. These are long-forgotten practices. Now if you cry, you're considered weak, so everyone holds back their tears; in so doing they follow to the letter the advice of one of their poets: "Be strong as you follow the road where destiny leads you." These are people who've accepted death as a fact of nature—no more, no less. As a result, it's been degraded. It has no special significance and no semblance of victory to call its own. They proceed in silence so as to show that if Death lives, it's because people die. It's a completely different view of life than what we have. However, we do think alike in numerous instances.

WATCHED AS a group of Anglo-Saxons descended from their ganglion of a tourist bus to rub shoulders with the Parisians. Whether there's a crowd or not, they always walk at the same majestic pace, like camels crossing a desert. They take deep puffs on their cigars, and the expression on their faces is almost always somber. The city is literally impregnated with them. And it values their somberness even though others see them as haughty and indifferent. As I watched these tourists, I realized just how naive I'd been; yes, my friend, I'd misjudged the Parisians, those strange beings who carry their right to free speech so far that they even criticize themselves. Yes, I admit it. And at the risk of causing a scandal or being struck by lightning, or even thought loony, I take my stand: the Parisians don't run after all. Having inherited and absorbed the experiences of a millennium, they follow to the letter the maxim their parents have repeated to them from the cradle on: "Nothing is served by running; know what you want, and go after it methodically." They're up before dawn, ready to go at the precise moment. Look at your watch and time them. You'll find they march to the rhythm of the second hand. Minutes are too slow for them.

Give them whatever kind of dial you want, and they only look at the tiniest needle. Impatient though they might be, however, they never try to do business between noon and two o'clock. Since none of them ever skipped school or took the long way around, which to us is second nature—an atavism, I'm sure—they don't know how to beat around the bush. Good students all, and having acquired the habit of watching the second hand early on, they don't even give you the chance to tell them how much you appreciate their call before they're giving you their greetings and regards and asking about your wife. Their eyes glued to their watch, they plunge right into the topic at hand and wonder through it all if they're wasting your time. When they have the information they need, they happily cry out, "Good things come to those who wait." Thank heavens the phone wasn't busy and they didn't have to wait an hour to reach you! For them, an hour is an eternity; they know that fabulous sums can disappear forever in that amount of time. After all, a moment lost can never be regained. They adore keeping in step with time; even more, they adore winning the race. That way they can enjoy the victory at their leisure. Despite their pace, the Parisians don't like to tire themselves out. The notion that time means profit is so ingrained in them that they've given the rather quaint name of "waiting room" to places where they can rest a moment. As far as they're concerned, nothing must be done at random, not even for the simple pleasure of feeling yourself move or to get rid of extra energy; each step must lead toward a goal. Born accountants, and having spent centuries building their famous monuments, they know for a fact that "Time ignores those who ignore time." Then again, they have such a keen notion of what freedom means that sometimes they want to break loose from time's oppressive tutelage. Since they know full well how precious time really is, they'd like to hold it on a leash while they try their best to dupe you into thinking that you must slow down. They themselves even slow down when they read their newspaper, take a walk, or look at a painting. Perhaps it's their way of showing us how brief our life on earth is. Yes, this too goes into the making of a Parisian—someone who's heartbroken if he arrives late and utterly desolate if he fails to show up and causes you to waste your time. Since time is money, affairs here move at a dizzy speed. It's as though those who've refused to pay have just paid up.

I mentioned that Parisians worship freedom so much they wouldn't think of robbing it from others. Certainly Paris would be the last place on earth to tolerate a dictator, even for a short period of time, no matter how much the gods loved and honored him. But on this point, some think the Parisians have a very short memory. I don't agree. They're a shrewd and intelligent people by nature. What else could they possibly be since they've managed to survive in this land of contradictions? Not ones to mix the napkins with the dishcloths, and always determined to be crystal clear about things, they prefer to watch and wait—but to wait in their own fashion; that is, to wait as they walk, for they don't like to be left without anything to do. Parisians may smile at a dictator, but they carefully take note of his acts so they can throw paving stones right over the barricades and watch them land on his head. And the stones are aligned in such a way that all these people have to do is bend over, pull them out, and throw them. Having lived through centuries of history, these stones know what they were meant for: to end up on the head of someone who's misjudged the Parisians' patience, poise, and sense of self-possession. And all this results from the fact that Paris has forever been a great intellectual center.

There's a section of the city known as the Latin Quarter, so named because it was here that teachers and students once spoke only Latin. It's situated on top of a hill named after Saint Geneviève and remains the city's high ground of matters spiritual and intellectual. Hills and mountains play the same role here as they do for us back home, for there the spirits live. Saint Geneviève was thought to be a shepherdess who watched over a flock of sheep. I find it a bit curious that in this country all the female saints to whom God is known to speak are shepherdesses, young girls who "wear their hearts on their sleeves." Some people say that Saint Geneviève, their patron saint, came from a family of means. Maybe though, in an effort to impress people, they're embellishing this story a bit too! Whatever, it's known that she was responsible for saving Paris on numerous occasions. People even say she had the ability to raise the dead and restore sight to the blind. And after she died, it's said that she was still able to perform miracles—it's not easy to shed that ability once it's become so ingrained in you. As the story goes, two hundred and fifty years after she died, the Normans appeared unexpectedly—she had fought those pirates before, when she was alive. Thinking she was indeed dead, they mustered their forces and planned to lay siege to Paris. The Parisians, who didn't have time to hide the statue of their saint, did what we would have done in similar circumstances: they brought it right up to where the fighting was taking place and said, "Protect yourself by protecting us." Once again she sent the Normans flying. As you can see, one can't toy around with these peoples' freedoms and get away with it! Vanquished, the Normans decided they were better off signing a peace treaty. They figured it was safer to stay in the boat than to go under. I think we'd agree they were wise in making this decision. The Parisians had such a strong love for Saint Geneviève that they didn't even give her the time to enjoy the blessings of heaven she had worked so hard for. Whatever the situation—floods or droughts, winds, wars, famines, or epidemics—they'd hurry to awaken the saint from her sleep. They also tell the story of Louis XI who, on his deathbed, twice had the saint paraded through the streets of the city. But what can a saint do, even a patron saint, when confronted with the higher orders of God? She could merely watch as death fulfilled its mission.

The king's head "touched the earth," just as those of his last subjects did. And it wasn't easy to help someone out of a grave and into heaven. You had to keep a vigil, followed by a period of fasting. Then on the appointed day, church bells everywhere rang out loud and clear so as to call the attention of all the saints to the event about to take place. Early that day, as protocol had long dictated, the other saints of Paris—Saint Magloire, Saint Marcel, Saint Merri, and Saint Opportune—gathered together at the Church of Saint Geneviève. A cortege made up of all the city's dignitaries left from there, followed by an immense crowd.

Paris has another saint: the warrior maiden named Joan of Arc. Two royal cousins became enemies because of a rivalry over love, and, as a result, the country split into two camps. A war raged for many many years. One faction allied itself with the English, and the other knew it had to fight the alliance at all costs. God figured the English had no business sticking their noses in a fight between people of the same country. Joan of Arc was keeping watch over her flock of sheep when God ordered her to kick the restless English out. She threw herself into the battle. Alas! She was burned at the stake as a witch for having let herself get wounded right in front of the gates of Saint Honoré's church, in Paris itself. As a result, bishops and Englishmen alike concluded that God hadn't really spoken to her, that it was all a trick. It's said that her soul changed into a white dove and that this dove flew up from the ashes and headed straight for heaven. You can find statues of her in many churches. She's the only warrior whose memory the peace-loving church honors. But I've never seen processions in her honor more joyous than the ones we have back home. Parisians, we must remember, show restraint in everything they do. I'm convinced, however, we'll be nothing more than nightingales if we insist on copying what other people do. For sure we've got to take control of things if we want to battle the modern superpowers, but does this mean we must destroy everything we are just to remain in their good graces? Must we always remain sweet-tempered schoolboys?

The Latin Quarter was destined to become a world-famous intellectual center from the time a certain Abelard of Nantes, whose first name was Peter (there're so many Peters to keep track of here!), found himself at odds with his colleagues at the cathedral school of Notre-Dame, where he had been awarded a lectureship. He took refuge on the hill of Saint Geneviève so that he could continue his teachings in rational theology, teachings that were completely different from those of Notre-Dame. A proponent of tolerance for one and all earned him the hatred of everyone who championed the old order. The Parisians of the time, who were also critical of authority, stood by him, and they too helped to make the sacred hill the Latin Quarter we know and love today. The only Latin the Parisians knew was that of the hill, the proof being that the Latin surviving from those days is a language of either the kitchen or the sacristy. The language had to descend the hill before it could be its real, original self.

Abelard, both poet and musician, was the rock upon which Love built her crowning work. He loved one woman only, Eloise, who, in turn, loved him a hundred times more. Despite the obstacles thrown in their way, the distances between them, and the mutilations he was forced to undergo, their love for each other burned so hot that it finally consumed them. As was their fervent hope, these star-crossed lovers now rest side by side, a testimony to love's constancy. Let's judge for ourselves.

Epistle addressed to Eloise:

If, in your heart, a spark of love remains,
I, your Abelard, can face Death's pains;
Before my crimes, I yield and now succumb,
Pray, see that at Paraclete one builds me a tomb.
Should your eyes then meet Death's dread repose,
May that same grave our two souls enclose.

Eloise's reply:

May the heavens continue to illuminate your days,
But should they extinguish light's warm rays,
Save but one grave for Abelard and his Eloise.
There, may our names be engraved; there let them be read;
And if to these sad places love's lovers are led
To visit our ashes one day,
With heads held low, they will bow our way,
"Ah!" they'll say, bathed in sweetest tears,
"Will the price of our love be as dear?"

Collections of some of the world's most beautiful poems are published here. But inside all those treasure troves found in libraries, where specialists keep watch, there might be only two hundred poems that are true pearls—veritable jewels, I should say. The poets write of roses and springtime, of elephants in forests, of jinni—and so much more! But you never read of Abelard and Eloise, whose verses are judged too sad and gloomy to fit into the collections of more lighthearted lyrical poetry. They're not bouncy enough—not enough dash. Furthermore, they're of another age—an age when people not only valued fidelity but had the time to love. Since then, it's been a different story. To be sure, it's still possible for men and women to appreciate each other, to enjoy what the other is and stands for, but people now seem more interested in racing after the one who gives them the most to worry about.

Back then, teachers gave their lessons outside. Students from all over the world came to absorb what enlightened Paris had to offer. When they arrived on the hill, they sat on straw mats. It made no difference where they sat, just as long as they could hear their masters. When they returned to their own homes, they naturally had to judge things through Parisian eyes. Did they become disillusioned with what home had to offer? Did they reach the point where they wanted to undo what Paris had done for them? I even admit to feeling a bit superior now, despite the fact that I never set foot in any class, talked to any famous person, or followed the enlightened path of the Sorbonne's illustrious professors. Yes, I spend my time in cafes or strolling along the boulevards, where you never earn a piece of parchment saying that you've learned something and are worth listening to. But don't I wear the same style of clothes Parisians wear? Haven't I seen the Seine, Notre-Dame Cathedral, the Louvre, the Tuilerie Gardens, and Versailles? Haven't I too lived in this city of light? I feel as though I've become another man and have forgotten those ordinary, everyday concerns you, my friend, are involved with. Forgotten? Well, that's until someone reminds me of them. It's as though you're lagging behind in an imaginary world somewhere; it's as though your concerns, your customs—and at times even our friendship —aren't real. I sometimes even wonder if your concerns are justified. As you can see, Paris gives one a whole other being, another way of thinking. It transforms you without warning.

The Pantheon is also located on this hill—the famous building where Parisians bury their most illustrious men. The tombs of Rousseau, Voltaire, Zola, and Hugo are all there, along with those of famous generals and field marshals, even those who fought for Napoleon. He, you remember, paraded the country's flag throughout Europe. His victories were so numerous you can't count them all without leaving out at least two or three. Unlike today's leading military minds, Napoleon rarely sacrificed his soldiers for his own ambition. He wanted to see those soldiers at his side. They were men of character, not mere sychophants, whose constant wailing and whining he would have hated. Moreover, he never abandoned them, even when the fighting was at its most ferocious. In fact, they're the ones who acted as barricades, who helped forge his glory at the expense of their own lives. Indeed, their sacrifices made this man the powerful general he was.

Napoleon's worst enemies were the English. They were of Norman extraction—those very same Normans the saints of Paris were forever fighting. Corsican by birth, Parisian by adoption, he never fell for the idea that it was better to surrender to the famous Calvary of Saint George, whose fighting skills were legendary, than it was to continue fighting; he never consented to lowering the flag, even when the English were all around him and dishing it out by the handful. His country, however, needed money. The English never forgave his proud refusal to give in; they never forgave his Gallic strength and determination, nor his Frankish honesty, nor his Corsican "deafness" when it came to appreciating the sweet music of their fine calvary. And their grudge against him grew bigger and bigger with each passing day. In time, though, Napoleon's star grew tired of shining; it finally closed its eyes, and that was the end. But how can one man, who, for so many years, was singly responsible for bringing such glory to his country's military, to its worlds of literature, medicine, religion, law, and diplomacy—in sum, to all the arts and sciences—not finally wear himself out? What had to happen did in fact happen. The English, who could never forgive his insolence, ended up confining this illustrious man to a small island. And the Parisians never swallowed this insult. In response, everywhere they could they put their emperor on a pedestal . . . These people who love to show their affection by kissing in full daylight, right in front of everyone, lead the most regulated lives imaginable. They obey the voice of their totem, the rooster, and awaken when he calls.

It's been said from time immemorial that "He who wants to live to be a hundred, rises when the rooster does." Yes, another proverb—one of those great treasures they no longer know what to do with. Unlike us, the Parisians can talk for hours on end without reciting even one. It's because they don't believe in them anymore. Two of these sayings they don't even acknowledge: "Good fortune comes while you sleep" and "He who pays his debts grows richer." The Parisians discovered what these really meant and threw them both in the same basket. Their contempt was such that they "no longer wash their dirty linen in private" but send it to a laundry instead. It's less tiring that way, and their daily pace proves it.

But just like us, Parisians eat with their fingers—but you should see them, my friend, they're horrible at it. As you know, there's a proper way to do it and an improper way. You're not supposed to lick them after each bite or use them on meat or fish. You're not supposed to watch others gobbling mouthful after mouthful, and you're most certainly not to pick and poke at your food as chickens do. You'd like to say to these people, "Don't gnaw at those bones like dogs," "Don't scratch the meat off them with your nails like birds of prey," but they'd come back at you with a variation on the rule. Put a fork between their fingers, and they'd no longer even know how to hold the bone . . . Poor dears!

Funny because it sounds backwards? what does that say about my cultural prejudices?

*   *

*   *

These people who don't remember how to hold a bone are the most complicated people on earth. They've arranged their life in such a way that no one can make heads or tails of it. In this country you never know when to wake up, when to sit, or who should go first. Nor do you know how to reply to those formulaic compliments that come to you from two or three directions at once and have two or three possible meanings. They strive for equilibrium, but their expressions assume the form of an equilateral. And yet they claim there's only one way to say a simple good morning. Who're they trying to kid when we know there're a thousand different ways to say good morning? The torch they carry around the world has opened our eyes, and we've learned that each year they add something new to their list of customs and traditions. They'd like to relieve themselves of some of these so as to appear more open and down-to-earth, but there're certain currents you can't fight. As a result, their language is enriched each day with new words approved and adopted by that venerable institution, the French Academy. They're allowed to say good morning to each other, good morning to an equal, good morning to a lady, to a superior, a domestic, or a tradesman. But the confusion comes with such phrases as "Please be assured of my kind consideration," "Please accept my best wishes," "With heartfelt gratitude," "With my deepest respect," "With warm regards," and "With eminent esteem." The result is a veritable jungle of formulas that has grown through the years—a jungle in which even the Parisians themselves get lost. I've seen them charge right into a letter, only to stop before they finish it. With arms crossed or a finger on their chin, they search the floor or the wall for the proper closing. Such a complicated etiquette is designed to make us think they've achieved the highest rank possible with regard to progress and what constitutes modern civilization. But, fortunately, it doesn't destroy the charm of the city's various districts, the best known and most explored of which, it seems to me, is Montmartre—it's even better known than some of the world's most famous ports. Tourists from every corner of the globe congregate there. If the Parisians weren't by nature so curious, they wouldn't even raise an eyebrow at all those foreigners who've come from the farthermost point in Germany as well as the United States! They're a noisy lot, to be sure, and each one of them is loaded down with camera equipment. The Parisians study them closely. There's no reason for them to take long trips; others come to them. And the tourists seem willing to accept the close scrutiny they're made to endure. If, when those tourists return home, they don't mention having seen Montmartre by day as well as by night, their own people will consider them sorely lacking in curiosity. How can one go to Paris and ignore Montmartre and Pigalle? All Paris would be called into question if that were the case, and Montmartre would be blamed. You can, however, enjoy yourselves in the other quarters too. It's just that some quarters are better known, since they've had more publicity. It may be a certain address, a certain special calling card, or familial connections that have grown over the years. Whatever the reason, it's impossible to forget Montmartre. Everyone takes a bit of Montmartre home with him; even more, everyone leaves a bit of himself there.

The huge church of the Sacred Heart (Sacre-Coeur) overlooks the area and casts a rather dim eye on the visitors, who're more interested in photographing her than they are in talking to the people. Monuments, it seems, are far more interesting than the residents. Parisians watch them out of the corner of their eye as they finish an espresso. They brood over their Montmartre and its good Sacre-Coeur as if to protect her from all those tour buses parked right under her nose. To the tourists, however, parking so close proves their good intentions. If by chance they happen to gather up some of the forbidden fruits of this historical site, it's not because their intentions are evil but, rather, because they are curious. They may have personal reasons for doing so, or perhaps they're goaded into doing it by some demonic need to conduct firsthand research, where evidence is needed for comparison. An adventurous person is not always a strong person, however. This, Sacre-Coeur knows well. That's why she closes her eyes to such advances. She knows that roses wither fast in our world and that some of the earth's wonders are often impossible to resist. To thank God in advance for pardoning the sins of one and all, many Parisians are called Théodore, Théophile, Dieudonné, and Emmanuel—names quite special to God because they attest to the affection the Parisians have for

109

him. I've yet to encounter any proverbial names here, like those we give to each other back home: Climbié, Katchidèba, Bégroubèhon, Binzème, and Motchian.[1] Obviously it would be very difficult for Saint Peter to direct a Théodore, Théophile, or Emmanuel anywhere but to paradise. I repeat: Parisians do nothing haphazardly. They hate to waste time, and that's why they're always preparing a place for themselves in heaven. And when all of us get there—only after accepting many sacrifices and enduring many hardships, to be sure—who'll be there waiting for us? The Parisians, of course. We'll find them at the bottom level, motioning us to keep climbing, to keep making progress. They'll want to enlighten us to things celestial. These are people who refuse to put their eggs all in one basket. They love the saying "A mouse that knows only one hole is soon taken."

Long ago the Gauls erected on top of Montmartre special altars to their barbaric gods. These were called dolmens. The Romans, whose gods were a bit more civilized, considered these dolmens an insult against their gods. Since Mars and Mercury were outraged, those faithful to them were obliged to take up arms as a way to reason with the Gauls, who thought it improper to raise temples to a god. According to them, a god didn't need a special dwelling place. The Gauls reasoned as we do. The Romans ended up defeating the Gauls, and once this happened, the Gauls were forced to surrender their position to Mars and Mercury who, for many many years, reigned over Montmartre. Much later (I still can't figure out how they count the years before the time of Jesus), anyway, long after the time of Christ, a certain pope sent a certain bishop by the name of Denis[2] to evangelize Paris; that is, to remind the Parisians that Jesus Christ, who had been born a number of years before, called them to eternal life. The Parisians aren't very good when it comes to saying their prayers. But if they aren't reciting their "Benedicite" and "Confiteor," it's because they think their ancestors have done enough in this area. They figure that since heaven is filled with inexhaustible riches, they can buy their prayers once they get there. Relying on famous biblical passages and equally famous Latin

1. "Someday," "Remember ahead of time," "I'm invincible," "No one knows me," and "That which is dear" (Dadié's note).

2. Denis, St. (3rd cent. A.D.), the traditional apostle of France and first bishop of Paris, was sent from Rome in c. 250 to preach the gospel to the Gauls. In Paris he made numerous proselytes. The Roman governor ordered Denis and two other Christians to be brought before him. As they continued firm in their faith, they were cruelly tortured and beheaded in 272 or 290. CBD, 372.

quotations, priests wear themselves out trying to prove the contrary. The Parisians, however, figure that since their own language has traveled around the world and has even been adopted by certain black people, God would definitely be able to understand it. The fact is, they no longer want to hear Latin. To the Parisian, Latin is an "imperialist" masquerading as a "Catholic"; it refuses to die as other languages have when they knew their time was over. Clinging for its life to candles, chasubles, and crosses, Latin—the official language of the Roman Church—continues to weather the times, however, and to keep all the other languages of the world submerged under the force of its holy water.

Bishop Denis and his two companions were arrested for reasons that still remain obscure, and subsequently they were considered martyrs by a people who, in good conscience, thought they were serving God by offering Him the blood of a bishop. The good bishop had his head cut off, but it's said that he stooped down and picked it up and then went to a fountain to wash it off before continuing on his way. You can imagine how startled the people were! They kept rubbing their eyes to make sure this was actually happening; meanwhile, the bishop kept on walking, his head in his hands. They called to him; the bishop, however, was harking to another call. This saintly man finally reached the town of Catulliacus, where he was welcomed with open arms by a people not only pious but also terribly brave. Afterward, the town became known as Saint-Denis, and this is where the kings were buried. The area also became known for a wonderful wine. One could say that it runs in the town's blood.

This beautiful legend, which back home would have swept an election, here (alas!) has many detractors, among whom are some very powerful personages who don't want the people to sleep standing up, to use their expression. They want proof for everything; that's why they don't believe in such stories. But then, how can descendants of the Goths and Visigoths believe in miracles when they doubt the existence of even God Himself? The Frank in them has always insisted on being heard, but to no avail; the other voices invariably win out, and, in this case, the majority wins. However, this explains why sometimes the Parisians give the impression they're being torn between conflicting emotions. They'll even find people to testify that the bishop couldn't possibly have carried his head for almost nine kilometers. His martyrdom, according to them, must have occurred somewhere else—in Catulliacus, for example—since no one here has the slightest memory of a dead

111

man being able to get up and walk. But this is, after all, a quarrel for the Parisians to resolve; we must be careful not to take sides. And yet, if someone were to ask, "What do you think?," I'd just smile. Since we don't have saints where I live, I couldn't possibly comment on how they act during and after death.

But it's a good question—let's face it!

I raise my glass and take a drink. I swallow my response, however, since the last thing I want to do is plunge into a history of the saints of Paris, none of whom is a relative of mine. Even though I don't entirely share his opinion, the person who asked the question would probably convince me that I don't understand a thing, and his sigh would tell me he was losing his patience. If, on the other hand, I agreed with him, he'd want to know more; he'd want to know precisely on what points I agree with him—yes, me. Undoubtedly, he assumes that I believe in spirits and ghosts, that I believe in witchcraft and other such "nonsense." You've simply got to know how to conduct yourself here. But it's the same back home. Certain phrases can trap you; certain smiles can lead you right into a whirlpool, one from which you may never escape.

assumptions

During the course of their long war, Catholics and Protestants fought a merciless battle at Saint-Denis. The Protestant god was younger and more inexperienced than the Catholics'; hence, the Catholics maintained the advantage. They were able to keep control of Saint-Denis, which meant that the kings who were buried there wouldn't fall into impious hands. The ruling powers didn't even turn over in their sleep to watch the combat, preferring instead to leave the outcome for the gods to decide. Here too the living were sacrificed for the dead. No matter where you are, it seems the dead always have control over the living. They transfer their anger to us as well as their need to be actively doing something. Saint-Denis, whose exploits are unique in the annals of history, remains one of the most popular saints. Many people have wanted him as the patron saint of their town. In fact, one of the main gates to the city of Paris and one of its suburbs are named after him. The farther you get from the capital, however, the more the name adopts and assimilates other forms and becomes Saint-Désir, Saint-Désiré, Saint-Didier, Saint-Dizier, and Saint-Dolay. But no one considers them the names of other saints. I'd like to believe this, but with language in constant evolution, you never know . . .

Montmartre is also the artists' quarter. The people know each other well and call one another by their first names. You see them laughingly slap each other on the shoulder and ram each other with their elbows as they clink glasses unceremoniously. They're definitely a part of Montmartre's free-spirited world, where time is something to enjoy. They could care less about the rules of etiquette and don't mind embarrassing themselves. No matter how limited their artistic talents are, they're never afraid to let you approach. In fact, they're quite hospitable. They're quick to embrace you and cover you with kisses. Foreigners who scorn this sort of behavior, this warmth, have given this wonderful quarter the reputation it has today. It's unfortunate.

[Love, in this country of restraints, is so unrestrained that it always ends with someone dying. Someone always loves too much, and they kill themselves. I don't understand. If a blazing hot sun were responsible for such excessive behavior, perhaps we could understand, but here, with the climate so temperate, such effusiveness seems a bit too much.] *Haha*

In this country, where charitable acts once were commonplace, everything was shared: joy, sorrow, even expenses. Saint Martin[3] set the example when he gave away his cloak. Since then, however, when people don't agree with each other or share the same ideas and resentments, divorce follows—or even worse, one party is eliminated. Here women aren't afraid to stand their ground against men—at times, aggressively so. They even share expenses. Although they wear a skirt, to them it's the same as wearing pants; the only difference is, they put it on over their heads. Most of them adore our naturally curly hair. And yet, some blacks take it upon themselves to give themselves a more Parisian look. Those women who've visited our country remember it nostalgically; others dream of sun and open spaces and forests, all of which they lack. They'd love to be able to leave what, to them, is a life of hell, but they forget that back where I come from life also has its share of misery, its share of people racing to beat the clock.

Yes, happy is the country where the sun shines!

I'm glad the sun shines, but even though it shines on peoples' sorrows, it somehow never warms peoples' hearts. I wonder what people would think if I said that out loud? Would they think we weren't happy? That nothing good comes from our sun? Yes, no matter where you are, things never run as smoothly as you'd like; there's always a

---

3. Martin, St. (c. 316–c. 400). He was educated at Pavia and served under Constantine and Julian. In about 360, he founded a monastery near Poitiers; but in 371–72 he was drawn by force from his retreat and made Bishop of Tours. Known as a worker of miracles, he attracted huge crowds of visitors. CBD, 856.

hitch of one sort or another. This is especially true for us back home, where the fires of extortion are fueled by the wind.

I thought the Parisians had broken certain habits; that's why I was surprised to discover that they too long after the good old days when their franc was worth but twenty cents. Life then was quite different from what it is today: worries and needs were fewer; money was less critical; accidents were rare; people seemed more united and happy to be so; and women were more motherly, more encouraging to those who were bashful. A mere shadow of what it was fifty years ago, money now dominates everyone's conversation. There never seems to be enough, since no one's ever satisfied. Is this why a waiter kept me waiting for two hours? Perhaps he didn't see the watch on my arm; or if he saw it, maybe he thought our time differed from Parisian time, even if the hands pointed to the same numbers. Well, I went into the restaurant, sat down, and signaled a waiter. He must not have liked the way I looked. I kept signaling. He came and took my order and then left. I waited.

"Waiter?"

"I'll be right with you, sir."

I finished my espresso. "Waiter?"

"I haven't forgotten you. . . . Your order will be ready in a moment."

Time passed. Others arrived. They were regular customers and were served immediately.

"Waiter, what time do you have?"

"We have the same time, sir," he responded after quickly glancing at the clock.

"I've been waiting a while now. . . . "

"I know, it's coming. . . . I'll be right with you."

Just down the street from this world-famous restaurant, which is known as much for its location as it is for its specialties, are nightclubs advertising striptease—to use the English word. Parisians, you see, lapse into English or Latin whenever they want to say something that's offensive to their delicate ears. That way, they're able to keep up appearances and, at the same time, maintain the purity of their language. As a result, the English, who exult over the fact that their language has invaded Paris, don't realize they've fallen into a trap . . . The photographs of nude women are frightfully explicit. I may like to look at beautiful bodies—as I do other beautiful things—but I dislike those intentionally provocative poses. Barkers stand at the entrances to these places and speak to you in English or Spanish. The shows are deliberately aimed at foreigners who've come to test their nerves' ability to resist temptation. As for me, I guess I'm causing quite a scandal here. People told me I would, but I didn't believe them. I'm only just now beginning to be aware of it. I'm one of those people who can't seem to find a drop of water in an entire ocean. Yes, my friend, I too walked around Pigalle, but no one even winked at me. I could see all those smiling faces of young women leaning out of windows . . . And yet, not one single invitation. Not even a "Psssst," or a come-hither look. For a time I followed one woman who had on a beautiful fur coat. Her hair was as white as cotton. People say they're born with hair like that. They're called blondes. Men prefer them to brunettes, whose hair is brown. But there's a third category: the redhead, whose hair is the color of flame. Men tend to be afraid of them since they're thought to have fiery tempers. In fact, when men are with them, they clear the immediate area to prevent the fire from spreading and try their best not to throw oil on the flames. But the Parisians have lost this battle, for those who've decided to dye their hair red have taken a position in the rear, and every day you find men walking right into the trap. Since the Parisian male doesn't want to lose face in any situation, he explains his defeat by saying, "Whatever women want, God wants." A rather fatalistic viewpoint, if you ask me, and Eastern to boot. The striptease shows keep beckoning me, and the barkers keep speaking to me in English and Spanish. I'm one of many who stroll along, but I feel very much alone in this boisterous section of Paris. And to make matters worse, the blonde in the fur coat has just hailed a taxi!

PARISIANS are exceptional people: individuals who, even when lost in thought, never take their feet off the pedals. I don't know how God managed to create them. If they're able to walk as fast as they do without tripping and maneuver so easily through even the densest of crowds, it must be because their feet have eyes. Yes, eyes, my friend, eyes they call "corns." In order to hide their feet from foreigners, they encase them in shoes. Can't you imagine the pain they're in? The only remedy would be to go barefoot. But those special eyes of theirs are afraid of the light. Just try to tell a Parisian to go barefoot and you'll see at once how hot under the collar they can get! The ailment continues to wreak havoc, even among important people, who opt to go by car rather than risk having someone step on their corns. Much money ends up in the hands of pharmacists, who undoubtedly have their own corns to worry about. And theirs too are probably in constant rebellion against the remedies they're forced to endure. I've yet to see one of these corns, and I know I'll return home without knowing just exactly what those eyes are the good Lord saw fit to attach to the feet of the Parisians and why it is these people seem so at ease when they move down a crowded boulevard.

The city is so large that everyone compares it to an ocean and says that the Parisians are expert swimmers. They must be, given their ability to move smoothly over the reefs that foreigners are forever bumping into. Of course, we can't forget that their ancestors were boatmen whose coat of arms was a sailing vessel tossing about in a storm. Make no mistake about it: that coat of arms breathed life. In fact, the vessel itself is an exact image of the stormy existence the Parisians once led. I don't think any other people on earth have suffered as much as they have.

Can you imagine a war lasting a hundred years? Well, these people experienced one. And in order to win their case, they had to give the judges money and spices. The people were constantly being splattered with mud the carriages would throw up as they passed; they were despised and ill-treated by those who happened to be in the good graces of their leaders; and at times they were even robbed of their bit of bread, their mug of wine, and their woolen socks just because that happened to be someone's pleasure at the moment.

Our kings would cut off our heads and arms. When one of them died, dozens and dozens of servants would be called upon to keep him company. We have proof of such torture; we also know a lot about the other things those in power—and their lackeys—dreamed up in order to make themselves feared. And yet, if we look closely at our past, especially during the time we had kings, I don't think we suffered as much as the Parisians did under theirs, who, as we know, were considered Christian. They were forced to endure mutilation, flogging, the iron collar, the rack, branding irons, the galleys, the wheel, being burnt at the stake, being quartered, even being buried alive. At one time, the city was full of prisons and gallows. Every important person had his own—kings, noblemen, bishops, abbots...Much literature remains from this period, and scholars continue to examine it. The people themselves are so thirsty for knowledge that the books don't remain on the shelves for long. Here, you don't find that indifference toward reading you do back home. Parisians know their past, and there are people here whose job it is to increase that knowledge every day. The more they know, the more self-confident they are. Their kings, like ours, tolerated absolutely no opposition. But despotism isn't just a royal malady—it affects all those who rise to power. Examples abound— you merely have to look around to see how true this is. Where we come from, democracy has taken on a strange color, one that casts a pall over our skies and increases the burdens of every individual. Sometimes people think that simply because a country is considered great, its ideas have far-reaching significance, that they've acquired the divine right to impose themselves on others. Paris, however, reduces everything to its proper size. Periodically, you'll even see them removing statues from their pedestals.

Once in a while a king who was truly Christian would offer God the chance to "cut the rope" on a man about to be hanged. But this would mean going against a royal or ecclesiastical decree. Consequently, the rope chosen was usually so new and so thick that they felt sure the Creator would approve of their verdict. Besides God, only a woman could obtain a pardon for a condemned man. She merely had to consent to marry him. Most of those condemned to die faced their sentence courageously, and a story is told about one of them who, about to be claimed by an exceedingly homely woman, shouted to the executioner, "Hang me now, my good fellow, now—I pray you!" This tells you something else about the Parisians: they prefer beautiful things.

But don't think for a minute that all those hangings were carried out arbitrarily. Absolutely not! Everything had to be done according to law. Thus, when it was determined that a certain admiral by the name of Coligny,[1] a Protestant, had been murdered and then strung up, all without benefit of trial, the whole affair had to be investigated. It was imperative that the truth be told, that the whole matter be arbitrated according to the long-established legal tradition, whose laws, however, were—and still are—often interpreted differently from what was originally intended. When the investigation was complete, the admiral was again sentenced to die. A dummy made in his likeness was dragged through the streets and hanged on the gallows at Montfaucon. That's called "righting a wrong." And there are countless other such instances here. To this day, the Parisians seem more interested in form than in substance. You can say whatever you want to provided you know how to say it, and how you say something varies from situation to situation. A wonderful retort can meet with hostility or rousing approval—you never know. But that's the way it is here. And to effectively hold your own, you've got to test your feelings and intuitions beforehand. Parisians are exacting only when it comes to other Parisians. With foreigners, their attitude seems to be, "They're unfamiliar with our customs." And they're always happy to congratulate you on your efforts to put yourself at their level. The problem is, to reach their level means abandoning your own values. Some Parisians are aware of this and will say to you, "For heaven's sake, be yourself!"

However, to be yourself in a world whose borders keep shifting, whose values keep getting lower and lower; a world in which you're asked to keep your eyes and ears closed, as well as your mouth, is to let yourself be led like a lamb to slaughter. Parisians are convinced that people everywhere are free to exercise the same rights they do. But only in Paris do the terms "tolerance" and "respect for human rights" have a clear, precise meaning. They abhor tyrants with every fiber of their being, and if you happen to mention that your rights go unrecognized, they'll immediately come to your defense. After all, their rights

1. Coligny, Gaspard de (1519–72), was a French Huguenot leader who distinguished himself in the wars of Francis I and Henry II. He was made admiral of France in 1552. Catherine de Medici, alarmed at the growing power of the Huguenots and at Coligny's ascendency over young Charles IX, determined to regain her power, and Coligny was one of the first victims in the massacre of St. Bartholomew on August 24, 1572. Coligny's great aim was to make the Huguenots a national party. CBD, 296.

were once restricted too. In fact, if Paris were to decide to gain control of another country, it would be to institute justice and liberty for everyone. It would be to break the chains that confine people, not to deliver new ones. Parisians have too much respect for people to ever hold them in contempt, and their sense of progress is too keen to let others lag behind. Moreover, they're too independent to let others get them involved in a situation where their honor might be tarnished.

But outside their own environment, Parisians are often seen in a different light. Their customs—indeed, their whole way of approaching things—can take you by surprise. I've heard that several who left for the colonies found the entire climate of human relations noxious at best. And since they're not ones to remain silent, they quite vociferously rejected anyone who accused them of being members of a bogus community defined by color and special interest groups. These are people who won't always do what you'd like them to, despite the fact that they're always boasting about having long arms.

Parisians who've acquired a certain prestige wear tiny colored ribbons in their left buttonhole. I've yet to figure out what all the colors refer to, but it seems that red's the most important. For some, acquiring a ribbon is what they worry about most. I don't know if they pay for the privilege of wearing them, but I find the value they attach to owning them a bit strange. Every time somebody gets one, there are those who're unhappy about it. I've been told that these ribbons are awarded on the basis of age or merit. Here, too, it seems that who you know, how long your arms are, and how great the fanfare is around certain names at the time of the awards dictate who gets what. This explains why some are unhappy, for Parisians dislike people who're promoted unfairly. They're like us in this way. In the metro one day, I saw people with as many as five ribbons in their buttonholes. Others barely even looked at them. As I've said before, these people are a curious breed! The more ribbons you have, the better you are! Those who wear the decorations are no different from anyone else, however: they walk and stand the same way, and they too get swept along by others awaiting their train connections. I wonder if anyone even notices the ribbons they wear.

Everyone feels at home in this sprawling city, largely because the people live in their own districts made in their own image. When foreigners decide to settle in Paris, they adapt easily to its habits and customs, so much so that when they leave they never forget them. And it's virtually impossible to leave without immediately wanting to return.

You're scarcely inside a boat or plane before you find yourself lamenting your hasty decision and longing for the city once more. In this way Paris is like a sorceress; we may try to escape but we keep coming back for more. You find Moorish cafes, Arabian cabarets, Afro-American nightclubs . . . Even though each has its own special clientele, they all get along happily with their Parisian counterparts. Those who frequently go out at night might even start in one place and end up in another. In fact, it's almost a ritual here not to let yourself mildew in one place. For example, the Arabians who've made Paris their home maintain many of their Near Eastern traditions. That's one of the strengths of this city, one of the reasons it's so impregnable. Those who defend the city do so by defending their own particular way of life, their own particular district—that's the Paris they know and love. If the Parisians weren't, in some fundamental sense, all artists, they would've collapsed under the weight of their history a long time ago. As you go from one area to another, you can't help but notice the layers upon layers of history marked in the earth and on walls, each of which has played its part in making the Parisians—without their even realizing it—what they are.

But what's most amazing is their eyes, especially the women's. Sometimes they have a look to kill; at other times they're as soft as velvet, and you think you can read their innermost thoughts. It seems they're forever looking at the Arch of Triumph, that symbol of what the Parisians call the "French miracle," a miracle that's made the city a second home for everyone. The women love to make themselves beautiful for their city; in that way Paris is one big garden, a garden unlike any other in the world in the pleasures it provides, the charms it offers.

And in an effort to maintain the look of eighteen-year-olds, they enclose their breasts—which, I might add, range in size from delicious small oranges to ripe, juicy coconuts—in brassieres whose names resemble poetry: "Little Pirate," "Jewel of Love," "An Invitation to Romance," "Songbird's Nest." Only the Parisians could think of names like these. Again, advantage Paris . . .

PARISIANS are like any other people; you can never say all there is to say about them. They overwhelm you, and it would be foolish to judge them as a group on the basis of only a few examples. I'm merely giving you a series of quick impressions—impressions that might be different from those of an African who'd lived here for years.

Some of what I say may even astonish them, since they're also swept up in a daily grind that I too am fighting in order to remain myself. My feet are even beginning to get corns. I keep trying to figure out how to maneuver through the crowds without bumping against people. I find myself running all the time, and some voice inside me keeps saying, Why are you running? But do you think I stop? Of course not! If I did, I'd become an obstacle to others. If you don't want to run, the only thing left to do is sit in a cafe and watch the others run. You can't be a part of a crowd and do whatever you want. One meteor sends you flying into another one, and that's how you move here. This human tide, rushing as it always does to reach who-knows-what shore, sweeps you into the metro or sends you flying to the banks of a boulevard. Yesterday, however, I discovered something else about the Parisians. They spend a good part of their time hidden away in apartments, where their life follows a strictly traditional course. This is what restaurant people try to relax a bit but end up making more complicated by insisting that people use numerous plates and numerous forks and spoons. There's one glass for water, another glass for the white wine that accompanies the fish course, and still two more: one for red wine and one for liqueur. There's even a special knife with a hook on the end of it for cheese. All this is done to circulate money and thereby beef up the economy. But let's face it: it's also done out of greed. Competition may be increased, but it only serves to separate the classes even more. Some lack everything, while others have so much they don't know what to do with it all.

With time, however, etiquette has lost some of its rigor, at least in certain situations. Rarely anymore do you find two people eating a pastry with a small silver spoon as they used to do. Now, almost everyone does as they wish. Parisians may seem to want to liberate themselves from all sorts of customs, but they don't always do so openly because they consider it a sacrilege to attack head-on centuries and centuries of tradition. If you don't want any wine, all you have to do is turn your glass upside down and put your hand on top of it. Despite their typewriters and other technical accomplishments, these people still resort to gestures—just like us. I've been told that the smell of flowers helps make food taste better. Well, you've got to admit that pleasant surroundings and a group of charming dinner companions make you eat more. I assure you, I speak from experience. A dish is passed from one person to another, according to plan. And everyone tries to avoid launching into a discussion of sensitive issues. Seating is organized around rigid hierarchical lines. After all, you don't invite someone to dinner and then disregard their title and position in society. I've since realized, my friend, just how simple and friendly our own life is—all of us seated around one huge dish, eating and talking, our children close by, and then at night getting together again to tell stories. All that disappears here, and we find ourselves following a set of rules as confining as the store-bought jackets we wear. A dish jumps from one person to another, and the host is the last one to serve himself. Too bad if there's nothing left. But rest assured, there's always something left. It's considered polite to deliberately leave for another the piece you would've liked best.

When it comes to eating, however, Parisians—who fight tooth and nail to have all the covers for themselves—act as though they're solving a Chinese puzzle when they try to figure out just which piece of meat the one on their right or left would prefer! You'd think the others would come to the rescue. But no! They continue chatting away, leaving you with the difficult task of deciding for them. The dish makes another pass. This time around, you raise your hand and say, "No thank you," even if you'd adore another spoonful. What if the lady of the house insists? You still must refuse, but politely so; that is, you refuse in such a way that, if she insists you have some more, you're ready to concede. Do you ever eat your fill if you have to make all these calculations? Well, in certain situations, you fill up on etiquette instead.

As soon as you swallow your first bite, you must begin singing the lady's praises. You must constantly say, "This is delicious!," even at the risk of swallowing the wrong way. This tells her that you appreciate the pains she went through to please you. Whether you like something is of such enormous concern in a restaurant that each time a waiter passes your table, he always asks, "Do you like it?" He wants to make sure you appreciate the cuisine that's made the restaurant so famous.

He also wants you to tell other people about it. When he asks you this, you must respond, "It's excellent!," and then take a bite to show him you mean what you say. The waiter leaves, convinced that the food lives up to its reputation and that the restaurant warrants the front-page publicity it usually gets. Most people order veal cutlets. I'm not exactly sure what they are, but every time someone asks for them in a restaurant, the waiter always replies, "I'm sorry, we're all out of veal." It must be the national dish. They give such elaborate names to the simplest of dishes that I wanted to find out just what a veal cutlet tasted like. Evidently, I may not be able to.

I love to watch these people drink. There's a certain I-don't-know-what that makes their simplest gestures absolutely charming. They raise their glasses slowly and carefully toward their mouths; then they stick out their tongues ever so slightly, only to withdraw them again. You wonder how in the world they're able to quench their thirst when they neglect the most satisfying pleasure of all: trying to empty in one gulp a glass of iced coffee.

You get the feeling that the Parisians would love to air out their customs—to modernize them and give them a new perfume to wear; but who would dare take it upon himself to start such a dangerous precedent? After all, aren't the old ways rather like the stone walls enclosing a dam? Remove one stone, and the whole edifice crumbles. Moreover, in certain situations, they'd never consent to break tradition. To keep up-to-date, they frequently rely on a whole cadre of historians.

Caught between a tyrannical past and a present that, in many ways, threatens to be as domineering, the Parisians are forever hesitating between what they should and should not do. Meanwhile, opportunities open up, only to go begging. You wonder if they do this precisely to create more difficulties for themselves, if they aren't too preoccupied with what's behind the scene. But it's their nature to weigh everything.

This attitude extends even to those in government, who're so concerned with pleasing everyone—everyone, that is, who tries to obey the law by finding a way around it—that they pass legislation riddled with exceptions. The strongest are those who're, indeed, masters in the art of circumvention, since, for all intents and purposes, they take the law in their own hands. The situation seems hopeless. One cabinet falls, and another takes its place. In order to provide continuity in the world of politics, to show a respect for the past, some of the previous cabinet members are retained; they simply change seats and towels. Sometimes those don't even change. The new cabinet takes control by proposing old solutions that sound new to new situations that are, in fact, old. You're wrong, however, if you think everyone approves of such methods. There's a whole group of Parisians who talk of a complete renovation of the political system. Should that happen, let's hope those who take over don't fall into the same old habits that plague most nations; let's hope they have enough character to keep the interest of the majority uppermost in their minds. With God's help, they might. Meanwhile, I stand with the people.

If they hesitate to act, it's because certain people who fear change need to be accommodated and reassured; moreover, various interest groups must first be reconciled before they set their hopes on something different. Nothing in this country is decided by chance. Everything is studied up one end and down the other. For sure, something can happen to destroy the best of plans, but at least their consciences won't bother them if they've acted in good faith.

I haven't the slightest idea what those in power live on. All of them seem to have glowing good looks and a ready smile. I do know, however, that some have earned special attention because they make a practice of befriending people of influence. Parisians adore satirizing them. But they don't seem to care. The only thing they're concerned with is getting what they want. In that way, they resemble those loud-mouthed busybodies who congregate around our leaders. Like faithful shadows or watchdogs, they know how to force their friendship on someone and make it pay dearly. Since their greatest merit is not to have any opinion other than that of their "master," they're always the first to arrive in the race for seats. Furthermore, my friend, these people, who surround themselves with only their own kind as though they'd die if they associated with anyone else, have just discovered that tobacco contains a deadly poison. They all know it, but they smoke constantly, from morning to night. Maybe they're tired of living. And maybe because of this, death has mercy on them. And yet, given the fact that they're such strange creatures, what else can you expect? They're so determined to defy death that the first thing they offer a friend is a cigarette. It's their way of testing you. The same is true of alcohol, since to condemn its use, verbally or in writing, would destroy the national economy. Yes, these people may be free, but they know how to use that freedom so as to appear like everyone else. They've installed clocks in strategic places and have set their own watches accordingly. That way, they can move at their own speed; otherwise, they wouldn't move at all. In its race with the rest of the world, Paris can't tolerate any stragglers. Factories work feverishly day and night to bombard the world with both old and new products. After all, in this day and age a minute lost spells a corresponding deficit in the national budget. Parisians have such a keen business sense that they let absolutely nothing slip by them.

Despite their weather-beaten exteriors, however, they have the same worry we do, namely: how to defeat death. In fact, it's almost as though everything they do has that one precise goal. For them, survival means being constantly on the move and giving their all, no matter what. They may put on a happy face, but you find them in front of bookstores, staring longingly at works entitled "How to Live to Be a Hundred." Alas, not everyone lives to be a hundred, for with every passing day, one or two or three are taken to the cemetery. Their cemeteries, which, by the way, are located right in the middle of the city, are amazingly clean and well kept. Everywhere you look, there're flowers and marble tombstones. Parisians may not weep over their dead, but they certainly do honor them by erecting lavish monuments. You can't help but be acutely aware of the fine line that separates life and death. One small step, and there you are: in another world where, this time, you're the one who's surrounded by the living. Life remains so exuberant, so precious and pervasive here that it gives the dead free access to the city instead of relegating them to an area outside of town. In effect, Paris has adopted death and made it as thriving a business as those you find in the suburbs. Lovers are found in those cemeteries, lovers who've chosen the dead as witnesses to their eternal devotion. The largest cemetery in Paris is called Père-Lachaise.[1] That's where most of the famous people are buried. And it costs dearly to be buried here. Yes, my friend, money fuels the empire even as far as dictating the price of a cemetery plot. There are several famous monuments here, including the "Mur des Fédérés," a large wall honoring the Communards who were shot here in 1871. I can understand why some had no difficulty in accepting death: they knew they'd always be remembered. Their names are engraved on the wall in gold letters, and small flowers indicate where they fell or where their remains are buried. They understood the true meaning of sacrifice. That's what marks the greatness of these people, what makes the nation so formidable.

---

1. Père-Lachaise is the largest of the three Paris cemeteries. It was established in 1804 and named after Louis XIV's confessor. Among the famous personages buried here are Molière, Honoré de Balzac, Georges Bizet, Oscar Wilde, Alfred de Musset, Chopin, and Proust.

I came across a building I initially took to be a chapel since it had all the aspects of one. Alas, it was a crematorium. Yes, they burn bodies here. The ashes are gathered up and deposited in urns, which are then placed in a special vault called a columbarium. You find more women than you do men in this cemetery. Does that mean a woman's love is stronger than a man's? To reduce people to ashes and then dump them in a jar just goes to show how truly small we are in the great scheme of things.

How many dreams, how many hopes and plans are found in those urns! And what a frightening lesson for us all!

As soon as Parisians find an apartment, they immediately measure off the space available and set about furnishing it. They visit those who deal in tables, buffets, closets, and paintings. Since the Seine once occupied too much space, they developed a system of canals to satisfy the demands of both fishermen and pedestrians. Accustomed to carrying around a ruler and compass, of budgeting down to the last penny—in sum, of endless calculation—Parisians have managed to isolate themselves from others. Solitude is so prevalent in this city of perpetual motion that newspapers devote much attention to matters of the heart. Women explain how they've been deceived and seek advice; men look for companions who're "sweet, likable, intelligent, and understanding, who know how to keep house and how to make those around them happy." It seems the Parisians want to make their lives less businesslike and more passionate. They may, indeed, have centuries of remarkable history behind them, but their hearts remain the same as anyone else's. They too seek tranquility in their lives; they too want a loving family, affection and respect from their children, and sympathy and understanding from friends. Even if they have the enviable advantage of knowing the special role they play in their own history as well as that of the world, they're just as interested in finding true happiness as we are—in fact, avidly so.

Poets at heart, Parisians love to escape from their city and mingle with nature. They love sitting by a babbling brook, listening to the birds sing and to the wind rustling through the trees.

Yes, Paris is a marvelous city, a city where—if given the chance—love can truly blossom. But a certain innate reserve holds sway over the desire to let go; for the most part, people cling to a life of solitude that remains empty of emotion. One of the tragedies to witness here is simply this: because they make plans for an evening's entertainment weeks in advance, the least little thing that goes wrong can throw them for an utter loop and ruin an otherwise lovely night out.

I've walked so much my feet hurt. Who knows how many kilometers I've covered during the two weeks I've been here? I know I won't be able to see everything; in fact, I barely even know the area I live in. Of course, it doesn't help for the stores to keep changing their window displays. No, my friend, this country that creates new songs and a complete new repertory of dance steps with each passing season doesn't let itself be known as easily as one might think. You can't begin to budge those old gray stones, and you certainly can't treat these people as though you're one of them. They've had time to figure out who they are and can present whatever face they want whenever they want. After all, isn't this country famous for its makeup? And speaking of makeup, the women here are true works of art.

Parisian men are exceedingly tolerant of certain things, but when it comes to girls who have children out of wedlock, they're absolutely intransigent. What we joyfully accept as a matter of course is, for them, a total calamity. A child born out of wedlock is considered a fraud; an uninvited guest. In this respect, these men think a lot like several parish priests I know, who set aside certain days for the express purpose of baptizing children born of parents who aren't married in the eyes of the Church. You can't help but wonder whether the souls of those children born with and without the blessings of the Church are the same in the eyes of the Creator.

Parisians hate being stared at. As soon as your eyes meet theirs, they look the other way. I presume they don't want others to read what they're thinking. But isn't it more like barring the door against someone you know?

The Parisians, however, retain the same affection for us their ancestors had when it was fashionable for everyone to have a Negro servant. I can assure you it's truly a pleasure for them to welcome us. Even more, those who, back home, wouldn't dare invite us to dinner, here, on the other hand, are the first to do so. They want everyone to see how broadminded they are and, at the same time, show those others how wrong they've been. It must be the Parisian climate; it has a special effect on what people think and do.

Whenever I tell a Parisian that one of their kind from such and such a place back home behaves differently from the way people do here, he looks at me as though I've lost my head. But as we know, my friend, those outside this country often turn into absolute monsters when it

127

comes to administering one abuse after the other. Their own laws must weigh them down. Or perhaps it's the wide-open spaces that give them dizzy spells. I must admit we feel the same way when we find ourselves hemmed in on all sides by buildings that don't have courtyards, much less a view of the horizon. Yes, Paris constricts us.

Here you find people who've never been forced to hike overland for hours on end, much less face an enemy head on, and yet they're always "making an escape."[2] They conduct their affairs in the same way they talk and write—openly, honestly, and without fear of reprisal. They speak their mind, and the police, the gendarmes, and the judges respect them for it. But they still feel the need to "escape." No one says it's time for them to head home; instead they say they must escape. "I must be off now," they tell you after they look at their watch. It's an incurable disease. They can't keep their eyes off the second hand; and as a result they're forever running an exhausting race against time. If, tomorrow, all the watches in Paris were to disappear, the people would be so disoriented they'd keel over and die. For them, life without a watch would be the same as life without love.

I keep studying them, and the more I do, the more aware I am of the distance between us. They're white, I'm black—it's like day and night. And yet I can't help but wonder whether God intentionally made people different colors so that we'd all want to take the time to know each other. Why, though, is the color of one's skin such a difficult barrier to overcome? Haven't we all, at one time or another, brooded over another's tears, another's smile? Haven't we all—every single one of us—admitted to ourselves that all people are alike? We keep talking about different customs, different countries, different cultures, and different races, but in the final analysis isn't everyone the same? Doesn't everyone have the same needs, the same hopes and dreams? Is there something happening to me here that I'm completely unaware of? Although the moments of true warmth may be fleeting, they'll remain locked in my heart. And the friendships I've established will last a lifetime.

Given the importance of flowers in the daily life of these people, one might just as easily call this a country in perpetual bloom. Their altars are covered with them. Along with their faith, flowers are the most precious thing they have to give to the Creator. If they're invited out, Parisians always bring the mistress of the house a bouquet of flowers.

2. In French, the term is *se sauver,* which also means to save oneself.

Poets associate them with the highest form of love and are forever singing their praises. One of them once wrote, "A flower is morning's child, the breath of spring, a maiden's grace, the source of all perfume, and a poet's dearest love." The kings even had flowers on their coats of arms. The people here who say you should never hit a woman, even with a rose, are the very same ones who openly exhort the people not to pay higher taxes if they themselves haven't agreed to do so. The strange thing is, everyone finds this perfectly normal. Back home, the powers that be would've taken this as a call to riot if not to revolt. Maybe it's the sun that causes us to lose our tempers so easily. Who knows? But in our country, aren't we forbidden to take a position contrary to that established by those in political power? And yet, if we did, would the sheer strength of our numbers force them into silent obscurity? The Parisians just smile when I tell them this. Having overcome all those who tried to dash their hopes and break their spirit, they know what people must go through to win their rights. Throughout their long and glorious history, they've waged a constant battle to have their own voice count for something, to earn the right to control their own destinies.

You can't believe the amicable relationship that exists between taxi-drivers and pedestrians. Not one single accident, and God knows the incredible number of cars that race through the streets here! If we went at this speed back home, every single pedestrian would have been exterminated long ago! I've yet to hear a driver curse the way some of ours do: "Go ahead, kill him! His insurance will pay!" Some even think they can do anything they want, that pedestrians are no better than dogs. Since the taxi-drivers here don't even smoke, passengers aren't plagued by smoke and ashes flying in their faces. I've yet to figure out, though, when they have time to stop for gas and oil. It's an absolute pleasure riding in a taxi here, since everyone knows how valuable your time is. All you have to do is raise your little finger and murmur "hep," and a taxi will pull right up. Those drivers must have eyes in the back of their heads and ears that could hear a pin drop. And what amazing finesse when it comes to starting and stopping! With both hands on the steering wheel, they make a point of telling you what street and what monument you're passing at any given time. What they're really doing, however, is making sure you appreciate their splendid city. They've been told to "spread the word," and spread the word they do.

Are there any people in the world more disciplined than the Parisians? Their ancestors stormed a fortified prison and then marched on Versailles to capture a king and queen; they willingly—and quietly—line up for the bus or metro; they wait their turn when they enter a cinema, a restaurant, or a bank. One wonders if they're tired and conserving energy or merely holding back. The way they look at women, however, convinces me that all men are alike. They appreciate a well-endowed chest, a soft, velvetlike gaze, and beautiful skin, and they're completely captivated by a woman's perfume and the sound of her voice. Even the way a woman walks lures them like bait... My walk led me to the Colonial Office. A complete village unto itself. More like a citadel, I should say, but the people are courteous. Even the receptionists and secretaries are nice. The former may not know in precisely which department one can find a Mr. Durand, but they tell you what floor to try and even give you an office number. Later, when they see you leave, they wave goodbye, but in a way that makes you think they're sorry to see you go. You can't blame them if they don't know everyone there. It's a huge well-guarded building with enormous arched entryways. That's because Paris reigns supreme over a number of territories she's trying to bring into the twentieth century. It's a heavy burden, to be sure, but one that has a certain amount of prestige attached to it. You always feel a bit sad when a child grows up, for as soon as it learns how to fly on its own, you're left feeling a bit empty. Paris dreads this and wants to keep her children close by. She wants to watch over them, protect them while they're growing up. But like all children, these too want something else; they know that wisdom comes from learning to do things on their own. People accuse the Colonial Office of over-protection, of forcing itself on its children, thereby hindering their growth. They accuse it also of living in the past, of believing that every hand on every clock points toward Paris. We must admit that its calculations aren't always correct when it attempts to measure the prodigious forces set in motion by its actions. I wonder if the men who play whatever game they play in this place know what others say about them?... Ah, finally. Someone's coming to help me. I explain my situation—that I need his signature on my travel documents—and right away he signs the paper I hand him. I thank him. He shakes my hand and says, "At your service, sir." Back home, anyone in his position would've made me run from office to office to get a thousand and one different okay's before he signed. Would to God that all bureaucracies realized they existed to help people. Let's hope that day comes—and soon!

Paris! Everywhere I look I see gray walls... and more gray walls.

They're beginning to make me dizzy. I'm constantly being reminded of the past, Paris's past, and this makes me realize even more just how rootless I've become. Every day a little bit more of my own past fades away, much like an old man who dies and leaves nothing behind. My feet never touch earth here; I seem to just drift along. Yes, my friend, I've become acutely aware of this. . . . I'm now at the Invalides,[3] another famous landmark. On special occasions Parisians gather in the old church to hear mass. Old tanks and cannons line the entranceway, and everywhere you look there are tourists, crowds of them. Napoleon's buried here, and along with him the history of an entire empire. If we were to weigh this man's influence on human events, I'm sure it would equal that of a king—no, several kings, and maybe even more. The guide's voice is the best living proof you can find of the feelings these people still have for their emperor. To tell the truth, the guide sounded as though he could've been a soldier in Napoleon's Old Guard. His one wish is for people to appreciate what the emperor did, for them to love him as much as the Parisians do. I saw him cast an angry look at one tourist who was dragging his feet on the stairway leading to the crypt where Napoleon lies buried.

This church is called Saint-Louis des Invalides, and hanging all along the nave are flags captured in the wars of the nineteenth century. There are also several exposition rooms where you can relive the battles fought by the famous emperor. Everything's been carefully preserved. These are a tradition-loving people who'll never let themselves be defeated because they're always mindful of the need to preserve something that gives them faith in their destiny. Everyone needs to visit this country in order to understand the full significance of Paris's motto, *"Fluctuat nec mergitur."*[4] How true this statement is!

3. The Hotel des Invalides was built on the order of Louis XIV to house disabled soldiers. Government offices and an army museum occupy several wings. The church of Saint-Louis des Invalides is on the south side of the complex, and adjoining the church is the Dome des Invalides, which was built by Mansart between 1675 and 1706 and which houses the crypt containing Napoleon's tomb.

4. *"Fluctuat nec mergitur"* is the motto under the ship in full sail that appears on the coat of arms of Paris. The ship is the symbol of the city, or, more precisely, the old center of the city on the Ile-de-la-Cité, but it also symbolizes the merchant ships that traveled the Seine and to which Paris once owed its prosperity. Translated it means "It [the city] is tossed by the waves but does not go under." Dadié may also have in mind a comment Napoleon is credited with saying: "Victory belongs to the most persevering."

A special cult of hero worship seems to have developed around this emperor, even beyond the borders of Paris. But Paris has good reason to export some of its history; otherwise, the city would die under the weight of it all. You wonder just how much noise those workers hammering away on the pavement in the courtyard of the Invalides can stand before they themselves crack up. Let's face it, those stones will be around a lot longer than those men will. What I understand even less is why the tombs of certain famous people are left exposed to the weather. Is that a way to honor them? Or is it because the people want to punish them for having acted solely in their own interests? Whatever the reason, the pigeons continue to perch there, content in knowing that those men in bronze will always remain quiet.

At the Pantheon you can see everything.

At the Invalides you can't. The dead are still alive there and form a protective shield around their emperor.

EVERYONE touts the climate here as being either mild or temperate, but, alas, it shows no temperance whatsoever. This July it's been raining almost as much as it does back home. And when the sun comes back out, it's hotter than blazes! It's a capricious climate, temperamental at best, and you're forced to carry a raincoat whenever you go out.

The Parisians have learned through experience that it's important to maintain good health. They're constantly weighing and measuring themselves and checking their blood pressure. They weigh themselves before any trip they take, and when they return home they won't rest until they step on the scale. Sometimes they're happy when they discover they've gained several pounds; at other times they're devastated over the fact they've lost several ounces. They search anxiously for the cause. Yes, these are the same people who walk around with a gun in their pocket and threaten to kill themselves for some silly reason or another!

The women jealously guard what they call their "figure" and shrink from nothing to maintain it. Everyone wants to be pencil-thin. You'd think all Parisians had eyes only for bones—collarbones, cheekbones—and the more they protrude the better! Some women follow a rather strict diet of pills, tea, and exercise; they eat no dinner and drink no more than three glasses of water a day. There may be nothing Parisian women won't do to keep their figure, but the years have a way of stealing by, and people do get older. As for the men, their eyelids grow puffy and their eyes get redder and redder; their skin grows more transparent and, at the same time, becomes drier and more sensitive. In fact, it looks as though the slightest little scratch would tear right through it. Wrinkles form around the eyes, at the corners of the mouth, and on the forehead, and the chin begins to sag. The ravages of time are less noticeable, it seems, on women. That's because they wage a continual fight against life's wear and tear by spending hours upon hours filling those furrows that time carves on their beautiful cheeks. They're so adept at the art of makeup that it's not always easy to guess a woman's age. And that's one thing you'd better be careful of anyway! You show a complete lack of education when you ask a woman how old she is. A woman is as young as she feels! If, in fact, she's fifty but she feels as if she's twenty—she's twenty! That's all there is to it. But I wonder if men really understand this. They're constantly looking a woman over to see how fit she is—why they even count the number of crow's-feet she has. Guard your age well, dear ladies. Remember, you are flowers whose perfume can never fade.

The thing I admire most about these women is that they refuse to give in without a fight. No matter how hard time tries, they won't surrender easily. Rest assured that tomorrow they'll be as fresh and trim as they are today. Perhaps we've taught the Parisian woman to look at life in this way, for we too have learned how to keep fighting, even when we know we'll be defeated in the end. They proudly refuse to resign themselves to their fate, to place their own heads on the chopping block. I've no doubt that Parisian women are the most aggressive women in the world. They absolutely refuse to yield anything to time. And they know exactly what their role in life is: to brighten our existence and to remain forever the delightful flowers they are today—flowers whose perfume and soft whisperings keep us going. They perpetuate life, and they want to be happy and wrinkle-free while they're doing it.

Parisians are as concerned about their language as they are about anything else. A privileged few known as "the immortal ones" stand guard to make sure that nothing creeps in to contaminate its original purity. These are the venerable members of the French Academy. Those selected to the Academy are all rather old since Parisians value the wisdom of years—especially when it concerns something as important as one's language. Destroy a people's language and you destroy their very soul. The Parisians believe this with a passion.

The greatest pleasure you can give a Parisian is to talk to him in his own language—a language all Parisians love and adore. Since they've selected a group of wise old men to watch over it, you know they want to immortalize it. To speak this language is to become a part of their cultural heritage, in effect an extension of their very being, and when you become a part of them, you also share their concerns for human dignity. We may never know such pride since our own language is dying off and our roots keep rising a little bit more every day, much like those of a baobab tree left exposed after heavy rains. The fact that we've lost so much of our true identity must disturb the Parisians, who prefer to see us in our traditional masks. For them, everything we are—our laughter and tears, our hopes and fears, even the love we have for one another—seems truer if conveyed on a mask. Some, however, try to

134

know us through our literature and drama—those ways of expressing ourselves we're inclined to do best. But they tend to approach them in a manner that suits them, that satisfies their own critical bent, and this often results in misinterpretation. Even though we appreciate their efforts to get to know us—and our creative endeavors—it's difficult at times, especially when some of their fellow countrymen boast about never having read a single work written by a black.

Parisians are completely and totally absorbed in computations, statistics, and diagrams; their eyes are riveted to timetables. They want to know precisely when ships, planes, and trains are due to arrive, and when they're scheduled to depart. Production is what counts—it's their rallying cry. Whatever they do, they must do more!

What's especially admirable about these people, who demand so much of themselves, and for very good reason, is that they never require others to pay them homage. They abhor the fact that some countries have the childish notion that they must bow before them. If anyone knows the dangers that arise when people are forced into subservience, the Parisians do! Such relationships never last. Of all the great cities of the world, Paris, with its long-standing concern for human rights, must surely be the most humane. As I've said before, Parisians would be the last to want to enslave others.

They'll always be at war with those who think they must subjugate others to justify their own greatness, who're determined to shine like stars while thousands of others are left down below to suffocate on their own hopes and dreams.

What disturbs me, however, is the fact that some Parisians think we want to race into the future without making the necessary stops along the way. Such statements on the part of an otherwise terribly logical people scared me at first. But after mulling it over, I've come to the conclusion that the burdens of their own past make them think that way. It's the way an older person thinks. After all, how would Paris look if she forced us to return to the Middle Ages and relive the Crusades, let alone the age of Louis XIV and all those wars that form a part of her history? But we must remember not all Parisians think that way. And even more important, no matter how often feelings and conditions change, no matter how often people may find themselves betrayed, Paris will never forget her ultimate mission in life: to free all those who are oppressed. She holds steadfastly to this course.

Their unshakable faith can perhaps be explained by the fact that Parisians are a highly consistent people, a people who'll never give up the privileges they've earned over time. They value an individual's rights to such an extent they've even opened up certain professions to women. For example, women can be lawyers now—and you might be interested in knowing they refuse to let anyone use the term "lawyeress." It's as though they want to "feminize" the legal world, to put skirts on those who're frequently selected to turn the wheels of government. Dresses wouldn't work because they're always black and cut the same way men's suits are, but skirts and blouses, and the like . . . So as not to offend their male colleagues, however, women lawyers plead their cases without benefit of necklaces and earrings. And yet, in many ways, Parisians do suffer the weight of tradition. They're a difficult breed to fathom, but when you see them day in and day out stopping to admire the very same fountains along the Champs-Elysées, the very same street scenes, you could just as well say the opposite about them. Fights? They've seen thousands of them, but still they stop and watch. You might think they've too much wind in their sails to slow down, but they'll slacken their pace and take the time to listen before offering their own opinion.

As they sit in outdoor cafes—their own special domain—enjoying their favorite drink, they never tire of watching the passersby. There's always something new to see, something unusual to pique their interest. You can tell they're endowed with fertile imaginations, given the number of different advertisements and theater notices you see everywhere, and certainly given the incredible skill the women have to completely transform whatever environment they find themselves in.

Certain Parisian women, those who're called models, are given the special task of promoting one of Paris's main industries—the fashion industry. In fact, Paris is one of the fashion capitals of the world. And let me tell you, this industry has its share of pirates. Parisians put them in the same category they do burglars, and they're constantly trying to hunt them down. Every woman here would love to be a model. They go to special schools where they learn how to walk, how to smile, and how to turn—yes, how to turn, but in such a way that they never take their eyes off the men in the audience, especially husbands who're accompanying their wives. They're forever being followed by hordes of courtiers and photographers and designers, all of whom help to make them famous. They travel around the world and enjoy considerable prestige. And they're friends with some of the world's most important people. The seamstresses who work in the fashion houses are called midinettes, and their patron saint is Saint Catherine—the patron saint of spinsters. If a midinette reaches the age of twenty-five and still hasn't found a husband, she's said to "belong to Saint Catherine." Catherine is also the patron saint of theologians and philosophers—indeed, of all those who stubbornly refuse to follow the commandment God gave to all His creatures early on: "Be fruitful and multiply." What troubles me is that the very same people who refuse to obey His commandment will be among the most honored in paradise. The God of this country may not be able to make people do what they don't want to do. But won't He set fire to those who don't carry out His wishes? That view of God, however, clashes with the one we have. It's not surprising that an entire people have filled their towns and villages with belltowers and crucifixes —all in the hopes of pleasing God. One burning faith to light the funeral pyres! . . . Here every profession has its patron saint. Only the bureaucrats seem to be without one, or maybe they have so many they've lost track of the real one. And as we know, patrons in all forms are exceedingly sensitive when they think people have too much of a good thing. They get irritated easily . . . If you want to insult a Parisian, truly insult him, all you have to do is refuse to shake his hand when he politely offers you his. That's even more understandable when you consider the fact Parisians don't shake hands as often as we do. What to us is an ordinary, everyday gesture is for them a matter of protocol, one that's developed over the ages. A married woman, for example, must volunteer her hand before you kiss it. Also, you should never offer your hand to a superior, even if you're bubbling over with gratitude. Let him take the initiative. That's just the way it's done here. And I assure you these people will do anything not to break a sacred tradition.

When Parisians have time on their hands, they organize trips around their country. These are called "tours," and absolutely everyone participates. Hours upon hours go into planning a successful tour, and the entire country takes part. The only thing they argue about is whether to take a bathing suit!

Although the entire country adores watching television and reading magazines in order to keep up with the intimate details in the lives of their favorite heroes, I can't help but notice a certain apprehension in their eyes. Parisians are known for denying themselves certain enjoyments, and as a result they're filled with suppressed desires. They too wonder where all this technology is leading them—not only them, but the rest of the world—especially when they see images of people who're hungry and ill-clothed. But the machines keep turning and turning, and the whole country with them. It's like one big dizzying joyride. The great evil of this century is this constant push to produce as much as possible, to get richer and richer. Man has become nothing more than a wheel, and he's provided with everything he needs to play that role, to keep spinning.

I get absolutely livid when I think of all the truly important human values that have knowingly and willingly been sacrificed to the utter detriment of all mankind. When I look at certain people, I can't help thinking, Yes, they could have invented something really special. But for some obscure and egotistical reason, society has forced them to turn a wheel instead.

God wants us to profit from the lessons Paris offers. But I doubt we will, given the fact that people everywhere want more and more. No one ever has enough since we've thrown restraint to the winds. We live in a time when fortunes are built without any regard for tomorrow. The philosophy seems to be "live for today." The politicians may say one thing, but they conceal their real intentions, and the people end up paying. And there isn't a songwriter in sight to tell us this, to help us break through the leaden atmosphere that surrounds us. As a result, those who live somewhere above the rest of us will continue to do so, while those who have nothing to pull them out of their lethargy will remain dull and lifeless . . .

Since the restaurant where I usually eat has closed for its annual holiday, I enter one nearby. The waiter helps me to a table and then brings me a menu. I make my selection.

"What would you like to drink? A good Beaujolais? Bordeaux? Or would you prefer a rosé?"

"Rosé, please."

I'd considered coffee, but those silver buckets on the other tables had caught my attention. Will he bring me an entire bottle in a silver bucket too? Probably. Well, what can I do? The cork was already off, and the wine was ready to be drunk, so I drank . . . right down to the dregs. Then, as the waiter stood at my table preparing my *sole-meunière,* he proceeded to remove the good parts—the sides that were a bit overcooked and the bones. Away they went! What a country, my friend, what a country! You never know what's going to happen next. In the meantime, an absolutely ravishing African woman—from the English-speaking part, I soon found out—came over and sat at a table near mine. She didn't speak French, and I don't understand English, so we just kept smiling at each other. You can't even make friends with someone the same color in this white man's land. And even if color did bring us together, other things would end up separating us. All the smiles in the world can't bridge that sort of gulf. Wouldn't you agree?

*

* *

I've searched in vain for the statue commemorating the person who had the wonderful idea of decongesting the streets of Paris by creating the metro, undoubtedly the easiest and most economical way to get around if you know the city fairly well. Its only drawback is that most of the tracks are underground. But that doesn't stop you. You're elbow to elbow with people whether you're in the corridors or on the trains, and this gives you a good idea of what life is like here. I'd even go so far as to say that in order to truly know the Parisians you've got to meet them in the metro, especially at rush hour.

I now know what all the arrows mean and have no problem jumping on or off the escalators. But once in a while I still get confused when I find myself in a particularly busy station. To avoid embarrassment, I simply exit and stroll along the boulevard until I find another station. The people continue to have that faraway look in their eyes. It's the look of people in a hurry, and it's utterly impossible to read what they're thinking. They're trapped in their own ivory towers, each pursuing his own dream. It's almost as though they've deliberately chosen to wear the coldhearted look of their houses and monuments. Most of the noise you hear comes from cars and trains, but footsteps add their share. You'd love to be able to figure these people out, and I wonder sometimes if that wouldn't be possible, given their willingness to help you learn your way around. Maybe they're only serious on the surface. Let's face it, they can't be down in the dumps all the time! I know for a fact they can't be. I've seen them suddenly break out in laughter, and when this happens they laugh almost as hard as we do. Nowhere in the world can you find more to amuse you than here. Paris is filled with entertainment of every sort. Their love for art in all its forms, their unquenchable thirst for knowledge—why, it's enough to make your head swim! The Parisians shrink from nothing. They have good heads on their shoulders, and their feet are so firmly planted on the ground that they never lose their bearings. Their doors may be closed, but they're not hermetically sealed. Paris simply demands something from you before she's willing to open up. It takes time and effort to know someone well, and that's why it's so important for people to keep talking to each other.

Two young women in a restaurant are reading *L'Humanité,* the working-class newspaper—more accurately, a communist newspaper. Communists are accused of making sinister plans to overthrow the present regime and install their own in its place. A rather primitive people who happen to find themselves smack dab in the middle of the twentieth century, these communists want to return to that period of time when people held things in common and, as a result, could touch elbows. Some might say they want to lead the sort of life we lead back home: a life they believe is far removed from the one found in the city, that they want to escape the constant noise and the feeling of being hemmed in by houses piled on top of one another, that they want to commune with nature. What those people who say this don't realize, however, is that our way of life has disintegrated over the years as a result of our contacts with other civilizations. Why, we don't even know where we're going to land since someone else is at the helm. We're floundering about in dangerous seas, and it's every man for himself! How many people will end up being sacrificed in this desperate race toward individualism—a doctrine even the Parisians are beginning to question?

The newspaper you read places you on the left, the right, or in the center. No one resents you on account of this, since the right to believe what you wish is clearly set forth in the constitution. They might try to get you to change your mind by staging a monstrous uproar, but they'll never question your right to speak. Left is red; right is clearly blue; center, white. And a whole passel of political parties is connected to each of these three colors. The very fact that you have so many different parties here testifies to the extraordinary vitality of these people. These parties can come together or go their separate ways; it all depends on the particular issues at any given moment. You don't join a party for petty or sordid reasons, nor do you join it to avoid controversy or simply to garner support for your own political agenda; you join it because you want a free and open exchange of ideas. And let me tell you, my friend, such exchanges are all the rage here! Those who read *L'Humanité* are called "reds" because their subversive ideas are the color of fire. These modern-day crusaders are trying to surround the city in scarlet. Thus far they're waging a peaceful war, but a continuous one. And the government is trying to keep them at bay since their ongoing activities threaten to overturn all those bibelots it's taken centuries to collect and arrange. They make no bones about wanting to take over the reigns of government and place a red-hot iron on all open wounds. In fact, everywhere they look they see nothing but people in pain. It's difficult trying to figure out how their eyes are made. And they're so powerful they've succeeded in having their color represented on the national flag. If you stop to think about it, you might honestly wonder if indeed this country will move in that direction since red is the last of the flag's three colors. Should they rearrange the colors? In what order? What about leaving red out entirely? After all, they keep making more and more noise, and as a result neither the "blues" nor the "whites" get any rest whatsoever. How about putting them in prison? They'd be even more cantankerous when they got out. They're troublesome boors, according to many, nothing but animals that should be rounded up and put in cages.

I haven't yet been able to differentiate a republican-democrat from a democrat-republican, a right-wing socialist from a left-wing socialist—in fact, it's hard to see the difference in any of those labels given to people in politics. But even though we may have difficulty distinguishing one from the other, they don't find it difficult at all. They simply give their product a different packaging and a different color. And they try their best to keep their distance from each other in order to make sure one color isn't confused with another.

<u>Politics is their greatest passion</u>. Some Parisians even make a career of it. To discourage them from doing this, others are forever calling them communists. But they must be invulnerable to such attacks, for nothing seems to slow them down. And life rolls on as it always has. I'm inclined to think that those who're attacking aim to the side so as to prolong the spectacle or let it change of its own accord . . . One of the women in the restaurant orders coffee, then opens her purse and begins to freshen her makeup. Parisian women always aim to be captivating, to present the best face possible. The walls surrounding them may be gray, but they want men to be forever young in heart and spirit; that's why they continually fight against old age, ankylosis, and death . . . She opens her newspaper again, eats a sandwich, and works a crossword puzzle. At another table, a young soldier sits in front of a glass of beer, studying away. These are people who want to do so many things at the same time . . .

*

* *

Paris isn't an easy place to get to know. Streets, avenues, suburbs, dead ends, boulevards, all the various districts—each has its own special character, its own special customs and history. People have passed through here for centuries, and each has left behind something of himself. How many dreams must have been born on those park benches! Certainly more than could be dreamed in a few days . . .

The more unattractive the women are the grumpier they become, especially if you smile. They think you're ridiculing them. This is certainly the case if those women happen to work in hotels. A student friend and I were looking for a room, and, as luck would have it, we stumbled upon two of those detestable creatures: a maid of indeterminate age and a proprietor of the same ilk. I hesitate to even say what I'm about to say, since Parisians will deny it, but from time to time—in cafes, restaurants, even in hotels—they pass gas . . . Well, after having undressed us with her eyes, this maid refused to let us see the two rooms the proprietor suggested were in our price range.

"But Madame . . ."

"Take it or leave it. We don't let just anyone who walks in the door see the rooms . . ."

"Is this the way to do business?"

"That's the way we do it here."

"What about those people who just left?"

"Tourists . . . it's different with them."

Her rudeness disarmed me. Then again, everyone who lives here is not a pedigreed Parisian. The problem is, people from all over the world have come to the city to work, and Paris simply hasn't had the time to polish everyone's manners. It's apparent they haven't been reimbursed for traveling from their provinces, let alone been granted a paid leave of absence. This is totally opposite from what we do back home when someone is sent from Guinea to the Ivory Coast or from the Ivory Coast to Dahomey. After all, when you go from Dakar to Abidjan, you're still in the same colony, so to speak. Moreover, in each one of our cities, you find rice from Kissidougou, cassava from Dahomey, corn from the Ivory Coast, and millet from the Soudan. The fruits of our labors. Parisians would collapse in utter disbelief if they knew we could get up to a year of paid leave . . . And this calls itself a first-class hotel! I can understand why the maid was so irritable. A face as black as mine questions her very existence, threatens every value she has—it couldn't possibly belong to a person of importance. I meet with the same attitude on almost every street corner. Still, the maid didn't have

142

to shout at me like that. But now I have a better understanding of the noise in our own cities—those teenage gangs hanging out every night . . . and the infernal racket made by all those motorcycles backfiring. Young kids who've lost their roots, who're growing up no longer knowing what to cling to for support. Everything around them has decayed, and they haven't yet had the time to substitute new values for the ones that have been destroyed. For the moment, they feel free; for the moment, the streets give them the space they need . . .

Knowing full well their city is populated with neither saints nor angels, Parisians manage to arrange things so that somewhere along the line, you'll meet up with someone, or something, whose function it is to keep you from losing your temper. It just so happened that a few steps down the street from that horrible hotel my friend and I first visited there was another one that welcomed us with open arms. You may have one bad experience, but Parisians try their best to make sure you don't have two. They'll do what they can to put you at ease—another point in their favor.

I've finally realized what distinguishes us most from these people. It hit me as I was watching the maid in the hotel I'm now in—a tiny little brunette with a very pleasant manner. During the first few days I was here she treated me with professional indifference. Slowly but surely, however, she became less distant, more approachable. A rather hefty increase in what I was tipping her made for faster service. I didn't even have to ring for breakfast; she'd bring it right up. We'd even chat a bit if she had "two minutes to spare." But I never got more than three packets of sugar—the usual three anyone gets. An African maid would've automatically upped the number, but here it's three, always three, not four. Everyone in this city counts on their fingers or in their head—never with their heart . . . Parisians may not consider themselves fetishists, but they are. They think that because they've replaced their wooden charms with bronze statues they've rid themselves of such primitive behavior. Granted, they don't say prayers to those statues or offer them something to drink, but don't they see to it that they're kept in good shape? Don't they illuminate them every night? Haven't they purposely set them in public squares and gardens? Here the gods are content to be the confidants of lovers, to watch the children play, and to listen to the dreams of old people. They keep an eye on the traffic below them and watch the tourists—those new idolaters—gather at their feet.

ALL STATE BUSINESS is conducted in a building I wasn't able to visit. Whenever a matter needs to be discussed, it's first put on a calendar. Then it's scheduled for hearing. The president and two aides preside over the debate. Each political party prepares its response, and the joust begins. Although the formal rules governing a debate are, for the most part, adhered to, some of those who've been elected to public office occasionally think they have the right to be a little more expressive, if not necessarily more civil—especially in such venerable surroundings.

Armed with a small bell, the president directs the proceedings and makes sure no one falls asleep or fails to see the significance of the issue. When it's apparent the debate is beginning to wind down, the president speaks. Here everyone's voice counts: if he shouts, he's sure to be heard. And nothing prevents him from saying what he wants to say—his ancestors have assured him of that right. Indeed, everyone has the right to be heard; everyone has something valuable to contribute to the discussion. Every party, every color, every group. A Parisian would never even consider saying to someone, "You're worthless!" After all, the simple fact they're Parisian means they're worth something. One by one, each elected official, whose voice is swollen with the voices of all those who put him in office, mounts the tribune to address the others, to explain his view of the problem. So many have been elected that the president gives each speaker a limited amount of time to state his party's position. That way, everyone, no matter how many prizes they might have won for their silver- or gold-plated oratory, carries the same weight. The country can rejoice in the fact that it continues to give the world lessons in wisdom and equality. I don't know if those elected have certain inherent privileges or even if their monthly telephone bills reach into the millions. I do know, however, that the people never let go of the leash around the necks of those they've put in office, for they know full well they're the ones who must pay the piper. They studiously examine everything their elected officials do and take solace in the fact that they can dismiss them if they so choose. If that happens, the ones still in power never go out of their way to help those who've met with disfavor. They stay right where they are and carry on with business as usual. The last thing they want to do is instigate a fight between one group of people and another. When I questioned the issue of awarding their elected officials certain perquisites, my Parisian informant swore up and down there was no such practice. I was forced to agree with him. After all, the Parisians' honor is not only a fundamental part of their city's glorious history but also the cornerstone of their motto, *"Fluctuat nec mergitur."* That's a Latin phrase. And here we have a good example of the universality of the Parisians: they're not at all shy about using foreign words and expressions—"football," "striptease," "wagon." . . . Paris even has a Place de l'Europe, a large square surrounded by a number of major thoroughfares, many of which are named after European capitals. The Parisians are convinced that someday all nations will unite under one banner. Let's hope with all our hearts they're right.

Place de l'Europe—the very name cries out for each nation to erase from its history and its monuments all references to having defeated others. Should that happen, history would no longer be a mere survey of those who've died, but simply a study of people. It would tell of their long struggle out of darkness, how they slowly rid themselves of all those pressures that made them treat their fellow human beings as enemies.

Despite the fact that they've also demonstrated their universality by speaking to God in Latin, Parisians are considered by many to be extremely nationalistic—almost to the point of being narrow-minded. They hate being accused of such chauvinism, especially those who're elected to run the government. They consider the love they bear for their country an enlightened love. But the president won't forget to use the bell if he has to. The debate must concern itself with national issues, which, of course, are the president's jurisdiction. The various political parties can discuss the issues; however, they'd better not try to sit at the head of the table. To do that would indicate the worst sort of upbringing.

Those elected officials have maintained the custom of banging on their desks and using as many witticisms as they can. In fact, the ones who tend to gain the most support are those who're the funniest and provoke the most laughter. It's as though the Parisians always prefer doing business with people who're young at heart; for them, old age is simply a veneer. Here, my friend, a good sense of humor is worth far more than wrinkles and white hair.

Even when things are in an uproar, people never lose sight of the issues being debated. You may think they're ready to burn each other in effigy, but you'll never find a group of people—divided though they may be on certain points—more solidly behind <u>national unity</u>. This must be the only country in the world where you'll find a revolutionist associating with a clergyman. Yes, my good friend, to show people that the battles fought between politics and religion will never sink the ship, no matter how strong their waves are, Barbès was compelled to shake hands with Rochechuart.[1] I should say, they met and linked arms in a metro station one day—all in the name of democracy.

As the Seine moves slowly along its narrow riverbed, Parisians rush on by, hungry, to be sure, but always determined to save their money . . . In order to show that justice reigns supreme over mere mortals, they've nailed an image of her on the front of the law courts. Those who, upon leaving the great hall, still feel they've been wronged, might find some consolation if they glance up at the figure of justice, for they'll find that her scales are more or less balanced. Parisians are so fastidious they demand that everything be explained through symbols. Often, only those who're quick-witted can understand what they mean.

Yesterday I was sitting in an outdoor cafe, talking politics with several friends from Africa—civil servants on leave. I had the feeling a thousand eyes and ears from all over Paris were tuned in to us, but I was more interested in what was going on right around me. A man sat alone at the table next to us; he wore a hat and held a cane between his legs. "A detective," whispered a North African, as he got up to leave. I told my friends that any government—I don't care what form it takes—should give a person a chance before they hang him. I detest the way people in power try to make others feel like slaves; no one has the right to impose themselves—or their ideas—on others.

It also occurred to me that, instead of relying on the sword, protector nations might find it more advantageous to look back to their own pasts; for if they did, I'm sure they'd have a better understanding of what their territories are truly concerned with. These are valid concerns, and if they were treated as such, those territories might become perma-

---

1. Barbès and Rochechuart are districts in the northern part of Paris, near Sacre-Coeur. Boulevards Barbès and Rochechuart are connected by the metro at station Barbes-Rochechuart. Rochechuart is one of the oldest family names in France, dating back to at least 980. Armand Barbès (1809–70), the son of wealthy land-owners from Guadeloupe, was, in 1827, a member of the then-clandestine Republican party. In 1839, and again in 1848–49, he took part in socialist uprisings. Barbès was arrested in 1849 and sentenced to life in prison. He was pardoned in 1854 and went into exile in Spain (1854–56). He died in Holland. (French Embassy, Washington, D.C.)

nent friends rather than eternal enemies. The most important thing is for all people to live in harmony, and the sooner this happens, the better off we'll all be. The man with the cane got up and, as he was leaving, handed me a folded piece of paper on which he had written, "Your ideas are well stated. Don't let yourselves follow the bad examples set by some. France can count on you . . . Thank you."

Funny country . . . back home, comments like this would be considered anti-French; here, on the other hand, in the very capital itself, a policeman—and I'm sure he was one—even congratulates me. It seems that geography has a way of influencing one's values . . .

You've got to admire the way in which Parisians talk about the life their ancestors led. They lay it all out—honestly and openly. It doesn't bother them in the least to say they used to eat from the same plate and live in straw huts. Nor are they embarrassed to admit that their city was once little more than an open sewer. They want you to see and admire all they've accomplished since then. But even today, they find their city dirty. We like the aged and graying look of Paris—in fact, that's one of the city's special features—but they'd prefer brighter, more sparkling colors. And yet, without those traces of the past, would Paris still be Paris? I wonder . . .

My stay here is almost over. I'll have to leave soon.

And wouldn't you know it? Just when I'm about to leave, the city decides to be even more enticing. Like a deceitful lover, she pulls you to her at the precise moment you think you're free.

Yes, my friend, I'd love to linger here a bit longer . . . I'd love to keep listening to the children babbling on in that wonderful way of theirs . . . to hear more of that mellifluous language—full of exceptions, to be sure—but utterly charming, especially when Parisians themselves bump up against one of those insurmountable problems left unanswered by the dictates of "correct and proper usage."

And speaking of language, Parisians are so careful with theirs that they'll only discuss serious matters between the fruit and cheese courses—that is, when their stomachs are full and their minds are at rest . . .

Yes, I must leave. I have no choice. But before I go, I need to buy a good raincoat. I went into one of those huge department stores whose catalogs literally shower us back home. Everywhere I looked there were windows and more windows . . . lights, escalators, people . . . A veritable beehive! Salesladies in blue blouses . . . one department after another after another . . . And what do you think I saw? Raffia, my friend, raffia from home—the kind you can't find in our own marketplaces. Let me tell you, these machine-loving people know a good thing when they see it! The salesladies never stop smiling—I'm sure they're paid to smile—in fact, it's probably included in the price of the merchandise. What a difference between the Parisian salesladies, whose very attentiveness forces you to buy something, and those cantankerous old women back home who get angry at the mere sight of you! You're lucky if they don't throw your purchases at you! The climate must weigh so heavily on them that it's killed every spark of life, including their smile. I'm not saying we should copy the Parisians; I'm simply saying there are certain things we can learn from them; namely, how to live and breathe freely and honestly, without fear of reprisal.

The salesman brought me ten different raincoats. He found something wrong with each one of them, some little thing I hadn't even noticed. Whenever I said, "This one suits me just fine," he'd answer, "I think the sleeves are too long. Let's try another one." You don't find this type of salesman back home. The ones here want to make sure you're satisfied before they take your money. But I had to make a decision, and I finally opted for one whose sleeves had to be shortened. When it came time to pay, the cashier, who already had one finger on the calculator, simply stared at me. I had given her a traveler's check.

"I'm sorry, sir, the store doesn't accept checks," she said.

"Why not, Madame?"

"Well, you understand . . . It's because . . . "

"But it's a traveler's check, Madame."

"I know, but as you can understand . . . We're not in the habit of . . . "

"Here's my identity card."

She practically snatched it from me and proceeded to examine my two faces, the one I was actually wearing and the one in the photo. I'm most certainly not a devil, but there're so many devils who appear to be angels that she felt it her duty to continue.

"We'll need your address, sir."

Precautions—that's the way it is in the business world. What amazed me most about all this was the fact that the cashier never stopped smiling. That made me feel as though she knew my check would be good all along. The Parisians are always on guard; they never take anything at face value, and you'll notice them counting and recounting any money they give you. This is especially true in banks, where they even hold the money up against the light. It's not so much that they're questioning your integrity, it's just that they want to make sure the money's not counterfeit.

I ventured into the lingerie department. Brassieres and panties in every imaginable color! This is where you see Parisian ingenuity at its commercial best. As they watched me make my way through the aisles, the salesladies started chuckling and motioning to one another. One—I noticed the wicked gleam in her eye—came toward me.

"Is there something I can help you with?" she asked, as she placed her hand on a pair of tight-fitting, light-colored pants. "Is there something here you like? . . . Perhaps I can help you decide."

I tell you right now, my friend, she definitely could've helped me with something! Anyone with her sort of charm doesn't even need to ask. She quickly realized what she'd just said and chose her words carefully: "I mean . . . perhaps I can help you make a selection."

The others began to laugh. After all, here was a man wandering around in female territory. You don't usually see this. Here the roles are reversed: men don't buy clothes for women, even though women buy shirts and ties for men. The women stay at home, and the men do the shopping. And they both do the cleaning and wash the dishes. Marriage for them is a shared venture, a relationship based on equality—maybe it's because each party enters the marriage equipped with a separate dowry, capital they can use when they decide to leave.

Several steps away from this department store, a traveling salesman was hawking an anti-corn remedy. Curious onlookers had gathered around him. Some went up even closer, looked at the stuff, and immediately left. Others were fascinated and stayed to hear what he had to say: "Ladies and gentlemen, thank you for your time. If I haven't convinced you to buy this product today, I'll certainly do so on Easter. . . . And if not Easter, then Trinity Sunday." This good man continued his oration, ignoring entirely the discussion taking place around him. He must attain his goal. Any offensive remark would send the people away. This is a good illustration of what the Parisian character is truly like: once these people make a decision, nothing deters them from seeing it through.

"Madame, this will cure corns."

"But I don't have any corns."

"Well, in that case, I'll have to tell your husband what beautiful ears[2] you have."

Here you have it—an example of Parisian wit at its best!

2. In French, the word for corn is *cor;* the word for body is *corps.* Since both words are pronounced the same, what becomes a wonderful pun in French is, unfortunately, lost in English.

And that's why Parisians love flowers and champagne and women—anything that excites their imaginations.

A little farther on, a woman is making some cardboard puppets dance; she calls them the "Marionettes of Paris." She gives a command, and they lie down or get up, pretend like they're boxing, separate, and box some more.

"Madame, I'd love to buy some, but do you think they'll understand my dialect?"

"Why of course! They're multilingual. Go ahead, see for yourself."

The puppets obeyed me. I bought four, but now they refuse to bow to my commands. Not far away from the charming puppet lady, a man is busily smearing his shirt with all sorts of different stains. He wants to prove firsthand that his spot remover is the best you can buy. It's fun watching him brush the stains off. He keeps brushing away, and all the time he's doing it, he's talking . . . explaining . . . trying to convince people to shell out some of their hard-earned money. He even tells them they can try the product right there and see how good it is for themselves. As you know, Parisians want to make sure something works before they buy it. . . . A few steps away a man is selling pens, a rather spiteful character who began by offering free pens to the first five people to raise their hands. Everyone's hand went up at once.

"Hold it! I said five."

Everyone's hand went up again.

"Well, it's obvious I'd better keep them to myself. I don't want to make anyone jealous. But since all of you have raised your hands, you must've heard just how wonderful these pens are. And let me tell you, they're known throughout the world! Given their reputation, you understand why I can't give them away. But they're only two hundred francs, ladies and gentlemen—an absolute steal! Come on now, who's first? I've more than ten left. . . . "

The city never sleeps. It's reached the age where it doesn't need an alarm clock.

It just keeps on racking its brains to come up with some new invention, some new way of keeping the world in suspense, of squeezing more and more money out of those strolling along its boulevards—tourists and Parisians alike. It wants to destroy the world with its ingenuity . . . its industry.

I now know why everyone in Paris kisses each other. Parisians were born under the sign of love. You feel their zest for life everywhere: in their works of art, even in the way they've arranged the flower beds at

Versailles—that emblem of glitter and glory that once almost ruined the city. It's the flowers perhaps more than anything else . . . you can never get your fill of them. Everything you encounter in the parks of this royal residence sends you into another world—a world of sweet dreams and equally sweet secrets—a world, in sum, of profound emotion—of walkways and water fountains, of woods where the sunlight shimmers on the leaves, of soft breezes playing against your face . . . You're aware of the very air you breathe, the smell of every flower, the sparkle in peoples' eyes . . . their smiles. . . . All this . . . and more. . . .

When you've seen Versailles, the Tuileries, the Louvre, and Vincennes,[3] you can understand why the people finally decided to take matters into their own hands. They'd had enough.

A person wasn't worth much in those days. But given the hatred that exists even today between people, I wonder if we haven't regressed. I don't say this simply because we rarely take the time to look each other in the eye; I say it because each of us believes that his way of life is better than another's, that his dreams are uniquely his own. We each think the other's past is not as glorious as ours, that someone else doesn't feel as deeply as we do. There's no disputing the fact that I'm different from the Parisian, and not simply because my skin is darker. We think differently too. Moreover, they're surrounded by all those mechanical toys few of us have—refrigerators, telephones. . . . Perhaps I should try to imitate them, but in some things I don't see any way we can close the gap that separates us. Just imagine someone killing himself over a pair of beautiful legs just because the body attached to those legs decided to terminate the relationship. He'll never be able to retrieve his love letters, let alone the clothing and jewelry he gave her! Sometimes all I need to do is look in the eyes of a man, woman, or child to see just how inane all those things that separate us really are!

Maybe people don't understand each other as they should because they've let their eyes see only a person's skin color and social status. Eyes that see no deeper soon become overcast.

When you eat out in this country, you pay a cover charge; it's included in your bill. Even if you return to the same restaurant a

3. Each of these was formerly a royal residence. Vincennes, like Versailles, was originally a hunting lodge. The castle, founded by Louis VII in 1164 and subsequently rebuilt many times, was the occasional home of Louis IX and Louis XIV. It's located about five miles east of Notre-Dame.

hundred times, you still pay for the same dishes you've eaten on before. It's just the way they do things here, and no one even dares to question this strange custom. I, however, find all this rather odd: when you go in, you're not told you'll pay for the glass you drink from; then, when you get ready to leave, you're forced to pay—"under cover." But it wouldn't do me any good to complain. The people here are used to such practices, and if I said anything to them, it would simply convince them I was from another age.

Parisians have been hit by an incurable disease; every one of them has a severe case of the fidgets. No one, however, pays any attention to this epidemic. It's made them want to build the biggest airplane in the world, the largest ship ever to sail the seas, the fastest train of all time. Parisians are forever hopping on trains, boats, planes, buses, and taxis. They're forever in motion—I'll bet they even walk in their sleep! Rarely do you see anyone taking a nap; in fact, almost never. I'm convinced they'd break down in utter exhaustion if they didn't have their various celebrations, if they suddenly found themselves without gardens and parks, libraries and bookstores and ferryboats—if they didn't stop once in a while and watch those slow-moving barges making their way up and down the Seine. The train stations are huge—and busy all hours of the day and night.

The people here have their own special way of saying goodbye. When a man leaves on a journey, he and his wife go by metro to the train station. The love each has for the other is firm and, as a result, makes such partings a bit easier than they otherwise might be. You see them hold hands and look at each other without saying a word; they take several steps, stop, and look at each other again. Then they put their arms around each other's waist, take a few more steps, and stop once more. They rub noses for a moment, then move their heads so they can be ear to ear and cheek to cheek. You can tell they're relishing every moment of each other's touch. Eyes closed, they kiss. Then they hug each other tightly, moving their heads first to the right, then to the left. This embrace is proof positive of the love they each feel. After this moment of passion, the woman rests her head on the man's shoulder, as if to put him in charge of her every hope and fear. They remain in that position—one against the other—refusing to pull themselves away, to be separated. It's as though they want to form a barricade against the adversity about to befall them. The man runs his fingers through the woman's hair, and she flicks him ever so gently with her fingers. . . . It's hard enough to leave Paris when you're by yourself! . . . As if to beg him to stay, the woman raises her eyes toward his—eyes filled with love. The train whistles for the last time. Monstrous timing on its part! The man hops aboard; the woman follows him for a moment, then stops and waves goodbye. . . . Here people don't wave handkerchiefs as they do back home. . . . She sheds no tears but merely descends to the metro and disappears from sight.

Alas! I too must say goodbye. It was impossible to see everything. . . . Indeed, I wonder if anyone can, for Paris is a complete universe unto itself. I feast my eyes one last time on a people who, like the poets they adore, are forever celebrating the beauty of flowers and women.

Yes, my friend, they love flowers so much they occasionally regret having but one wife—which proves, of course, that a wife isn't always the easiest person to get along with, even if she's called the angel of the hearth. And yet, even though their mistresses are named Rose, Mireille, or Christiane, they too have thorns. But Rose, Mireille, and Christiane will always remain sweet-smelling flowers; enchanting, magical beings whose every gesture, every smile turn the streets and boulevards into fairylands and the waters of the Seine into gleaming, shimmering jewels. They too add their voices to the magnificent concert that is Paris. Yes, my friend, Paris is all that—and more. And no one, absolutely no one, can resist her call.

With all good wishes,

Tanhoé Bertin
Paris, 14 July–2 August 1956